UNDERSTANDING

THE LORD'S PRAYER

PHILIP B. HARNER

Understanding
The Lord's
Prayer

FORTRESS PRESS   Philadelphia

COPYRIGHT © 1975 BY FORTRESS PRESS

Library of Congress Catalog Card Number 75-13035

ISBN 0-8006-1213-2

5106F75   Printed in U.S.A.   1-1213

To my wife
Willa Jean

Contents

Preface

This study of the Lord's Prayer is intended primarily for college and seminary students who are taking courses in the New Testament. Survey courses often need to be supplemented by materials that examine a specific topic in some detail. I hope that this book will help to fill that need. I hope too that the book will be useful for ministers, lay people in churches, and others who wish to review some of the recent developments in this area or are studying the Lord's Prayer for the first time.

The plan of the book follows the division of the Lord's Prayer into the address, the "thou" petitions, the "we" petitions, and the doxology. This plan will make the book useful for those who regard Luke's form of the prayer as original, as well as those who accept the authenticity of the longer form in Matthew. This arrangement will also make it possible to group together the petitions that are closely related to one another in form and content.

Interpretations of the Lord's Prayer differ widely, especially regarding the question whether it is eschatological or not. I have interpreted the prayer in the context of inaugurated eschatology, which is the view that Jesus regarded the kingdom of God as already partially present in his own ministry but still to come in its fullness. I have tried to give the reasons for this view in the discussion of the kingdom of God in Chapter Three.

Most of the book deals with the meaning of the Lord's Prayer itself, although a brief concluding chapter explores the relationship between the content of the prayer and the affirmations of post-Resurrection Christian faith. The appendix gives four Jewish prayers that very possibly existed in Jesus' own day. Apart from their intrinsic importance, I have included them as a way of making them more widely available to readers today. In the

Notes I have given the full bibliographical data for each reference the first time it is cited in each chapter.

The fact that the Lord's Prayer is so familiar may tend to obscure the need to examine it carefully and interpret it within the context of Jesus' ministry. I hope that this study will call attention to some of the issues that are involved in interpreting the prayer. At the same time I hope that the book will contribute to a fuller appreciation of the significance of the Lord's Prayer, which has been so central in Christian life and thought throughout the centuries.

I would like to express my appreciation to two institutions that graciously gave me permission to use their libraries, the University of Aarhus in Denmark and Western Theological Seminary in Holland, Michigan. I am also grateful to Heidelberg College for granting a study leave in the fall of 1970, when I first became interested in the Lord's Prayer as a research topic.

Chapter One

The Versions of the Prayer

The Lord's Prayer has been especially important throughout the centuries of Christian history. It is the only prayer that
Jesus himself gave to his followers. It is closely related to Jesus'
own ministry, for it reflects many of the ideas and themes that
he expressed in his teachings, sayings, and actions. It is rich in
meaning, for it refers to men's relationship to God, their relationship to one another, their understanding of history, and
their needs in daily life. It is brief and easily learned, yet it is
carefully composed and arranged in several sections that follow
one another in a logical development of thought. It is a prayer
of the Christian community, referring to "we" and "us," yet it
is appropriate for private as well as public use.

In this chapter we will examine the versions of the Lord's
Prayer in early Christian writings, its setting in these writings,
and its underlying structure. We will also consider the questions of the authenticity of the prayer, its original form, and its
original language. In some instances we will encounter problems for which there is no definite solution. But this type of
analysis will point to a number of issues that are important in
understanding the Lord's Prayer, and it will explain the approach to the prayer that will be followed in subsequent chapters.

The Versions of the Lord's Prayer

In the New Testament the Lord's Prayer appears in the Gospel of Matthew and the Gospel of Luke. The two versions are
very similar, although they differ somewhat in length and wording. Outside of the New Testament the Lord's Prayer also occurs in an early manual of church life known as the *Didache*.
This version of the prayer is very similar to the one in Matthew,

although it is not identical. In a similar way most of us today have learned the prayer in a form that resembles Matthew's version but is not quite the same.

The Gospels of Matthew and Luke, which were probably written around A.D. 80–95, give us the earliest written forms of the Lord's Prayer.[1] As a first step in interpreting the prayer, we may look at the similarities and differences between these two versions. The translation used here is the Revised Standard Version (RSV), with some changes in capitalization, punctuation, and spacing:

Our Father who art in heaven:	Father:
Hallowed be thy name, Thy kingdom come, Thy will be done, on earth as it is in heaven.	Hallowed be thy name, Thy kingdom come.

Give us this day our daily bread,
And forgive us our debts,
    as we also have forgiven our
        debtors,
And lead us not into temptation,
But deliver us from evil.
	Give us each day our daily bread,
	And forgive us our sins,
	    for we ourselves forgive everyone
	        who is indebted to us,
	And lead us not into temptation.

(Matt. 6:9–13)	(Luke 11:2–4)

It is clear that Matthew's form of the prayer is longer than Luke's at three places. At the beginning Matthew has a longer address to God: "Our Father who art in heaven," rather than simply "Father." At the end of the first group of petitions Matthew has a clause that is absent from Luke: "Thy will be done, on earth as it is in heaven." At the end of the second group of petitions Matthew has another clause that is absent from Luke: "But deliver us from evil." The additional material in Matthew appears at the end of the address, at the end of the first part of the prayer, and at the end of the second part. Later in this chapter we will discuss the problem of the original form of the prayer. As we shall see then, it may be significant that the additional material in Matthew's version appears at these three places in the prayer.

It is also important to notice that Luke's version is entirely contained within Matthew's. It follows the same sequence of ideas as in Matthew, and all of its clauses have parallels in Matthew. These similarities suggest that we are justified in regarding the two versions as forms of the same prayer rather than two different prayers. Most interpreters believe that Jesus gave the Lord's Prayer only once. A few believe that he gave it on two separate occasions, in slightly different forms, and that these forms are represented by the longer version in Matthew and the shorter one in Luke. Whatever the solution to this problem may be, it is important to recognize that we are dealing with essentially the same prayer in both versions.

The two forms of the prayer differ somewhat in wording as well as length. Matthew's version, for example, says "give us this day our daily bread," while Luke's version has "give us each day our daily bread." Another difference is that Matthew's form asks for forgiveness of "debts," while Luke's form prays for forgiveness of "sins." In the clause following the petition for forgiveness, Matthew uses "as" with a past tense: "as we also have forgiven our debtors." Luke, on the other hand, has "for" with a present tense: "for we ourselves forgive everyone who is indebted to us."

When we discuss the individual petitions, we will ask whether these differences are significant for understanding the meaning of the prayer. At this point we may notice that they do tell us something about the relationship between the two written forms of the prayer as we have them in the Gospels of Matthew and Luke. The differences in length and wording suggest that there is no direct connection between the two written versions. Matthew could hardly have copied the prayer directly from Luke, or Luke from Matthew. Nor is it likely that they both copied it directly from a common source. In any of these cases the two versions of the prayer would be much more alike than they actually are. Each writer must have had his own source for his version of the prayer. It is very possible that each one gives the prayer as it was generally used in his own church or area at the time.

The footnotes of the RSV contain some alternate readings and additional material that may also be important in interpreting the Lord's Prayer. Instead of "our daily bread," the footnotes read "our bread for the morrow." This is another possible way of translating the Greek word *epiousios*. The exact meaning of this word, unfortunately, is not known. In a similar way the footnote on the last petition in Matthew indicates that it may be translated "deliver us from the evil one" rather than "deliver us from evil." The Greek phrase here can be understood either as masculine ("the evil one") or neuter ("evil").

At the end of the prayer in Matthew the RSV footnote adds the doxology, "For thine is the kingdom and the power and the glory, forever. Amen." This doxology is familiar to Protestants, but Roman Catholics do not use it when they pray the Lord's Prayer. It appears in some early texts and translations of Matthew, but it is lacking in others. The RSV translators placed it in the footnotes because in their judgment there is insufficient textual evidence to regard it as an original part of the prayer.

The third early Christian writing in which the Lord's Prayer appears is the short manual known as the *Didache*. It contains a form of the prayer that is very similar to Matthew's. It differs primarily in three respects. It has "forgive us our debt" instead of "forgive us our debts." It uses the present tense in the clause "as we also forgive our debtors," instead of the past tense, "as we also have forgiven our debtors." Finally, it closes with a short form of the doxology, "For thine is the power and the glory, forever."

The section of the *Didache* that contains the Lord's Prayer is thought to have originated in Syria in the latter part of the first century or the early part of the second.[2] This was probably the same area in which the Gospel of Matthew had been written a generation or so earlier, and the writer of the *Didache* refers a number of times to Matthew. The differences between these two versions of the prayer indicate that the form in the *Didache* is not directly dependent on Matthew's version. It evidently reflects the way the prayer was actually recited in the area at this time. The differences between the two versions also suggest that the early Christians in Syria felt some freedom to use their own form of the prayer, since they knew Matthew's version but did not follow it exactly. The presence of the doxology in the *Didache's* version also indicates that the doxology in some form was attached to the prayer quite early, even if it did not originally belong to it.

The Setting of the Lord's Prayer in Early Christian Writings

So far we have been looking at the three versions of the Lord's Prayer that appear in Matthew, Luke, and the *Didache*, and we have noticed some of the issues that arise from a comparison of these versions. We may look now at the setting and function of the prayer in each of these documents. This analysis will suggest some of the ways in which the early Christians used and understood the Lord's Prayer.

Matthew gives the Lord's Prayer as part of Jesus' teaching in the Sermon on the Mount (chaps. 5–7). In particular, he includes it in a section dealing with the practice of almsgiving, prayer, and fasting (6:1–18). In each case Jesus tells his followers that they must observe these practices in private rather than in public. They must not be like the "hypocrites"—the Pharisees—who observe them in public to win approval from others. Within this series of instructions Jesus gives the Lord's Prayer as an example of a brief, sincere prayer that is suitable for his followers to use.

As Matthew understands it, the Lord's Prayer is probably addressed to those followers of Jesus who are Jewish in background. They are already familiar with the rich heritage of prayer in Judaism, and they have observed the practice of prayer all their lives. As followers of Jesus, they now need to learn that their prayers must be different from those of the Pharisees. They must offer prayers that are brief and sincere, free from any self-righteousness or public display of piety.

Luke also presents the Lord's Prayer as a prayer that Jesus gives to his followers, but otherwise the circumstances are quite different. According to Luke, Jesus himself was praying on one occasion, and when he had finished one of the disciples said to him, "Lord, teach us to pray, as John taught his disciples" (11:1). In response to this request Jesus gave the Lord's Prayer to his disciples. The prayer was to serve as a distinguishing characteristic of their group, just as the followers of John the Baptist evidently had their own prayer. In a similar way it was a frequent custom with Jewish teachers to use or compose a favorite form of prayer.[3]

The writer of the Gospel of Luke is Gentile rather than Jewish in background. He evidently thinks of the Lord's Prayer as especially meaningful for those followers of Jesus who are also Gentile in background. These people are not so familiar with the Jewish or Old Testament forms of prayer. In this sense they must learn how to pray for the first time. They receive the Lord's Prayer as the prayer that teaches them how to pray and at the same time serves as a hallmark of their life as a community.[4]

The *Didache* does not place the Lord's Prayer within any particular setting in Jesus' ministry. But it does include the prayer in a group of chapters that deal with the practices of baptism, fasting, prayer, and the Lord's Supper (chaps. 7–10). It regards baptism and the Lord's Supper as specific observances of the Christian community, and it treats fasting and prayer in a way that distinguishes them from similar Jewish practices. In this way the *Didache*, like Matthew and Luke, indicates that the Lord's Prayer was intended specifically for the followers of Jesus.

After the *Didache* gives the Lord's Prayer it adds, "Three times a day pray thus" (8:3). In this way it indicates that the use of the prayer should be a regular daily practice. In all probability the *Didache* is also contrasting the Christian use of the Lord's Prayer with the Jewish use of a prayer known as the Eighteen Benedictions, which the Jews recited every morning, afternoon, and evening.[5] Here again the *Didache* implies that the use of the Lord's Prayer is a hallmark of the Christian community.

Matthew, Luke, and the *Didache* all present the Lord's Prayer in ways that are still meaningful for Christians today.

Matthew gives the prayer as a model for those who are familiar with the practice of prayer but who may come to regard it as a routine formality. In this way he reflects his belief that prayer should always be a genuine experience of entering into the presence of God. Luke gives the prayer as an example for those who need to learn about the meaning and practice of prayer. His view calls attention to the importance of understanding the ideas and beliefs that are expressed in prayer. The *Didache* reflects the view that the regular practice of prayer enriches daily life. All three sources present the Lord's Prayer as a special prayer which Jesus gave to his followers as a distinguishing feature of their life as a community.

The Structure of the Lord's Prayer

We may turn now to the Lord's Prayer itself and look at the four parts that make up the entire prayer. For this purpose we may use the full form in Matthew, including the doxology. To indicate the relationship between Matthew's version and Luke's, the words and phrases in Matthew that have a parallel in Luke are underlined. Solid lines indicate exact parallels in the Greek text, while dotted lines indicate approximate parallels:

Address:	Our Father who art in heaven:
"Thou" petitions:	Hallowed be thy name, Thy kingdom come, Thy will be done, on earth as it is in heaven.

"We" petitions:	Give us this day our daily bread,
	And forgive us our debts,
	    as we also have forgiven our
	        debtors,
	And lead us not into temptation,
	But deliver us from evil.

Doxology:	For thine is the kingdom and the power and the glory forever. Amen.

This analysis makes it clear that the Lord's Prayer falls naturally into four parts. The address indicates that the prayer is directed to God as Father. The "thou" petitions refer to God himself, and the "we" petitions refer to the needs of the persons who are offering the prayer. The doxology concludes the prayer on a note of praise. It is especially important to notice that the versions of the prayer in Matthew and Luke, in spite of their differences, share the common pattern of address, "thou" petitions, and "we" petitions. The doxology appears in some early texts and translations of Matthew, but not of Luke.

A number of stylistic characteristics indicate that the "thou" petitions and the "we" petitions form two distinct divisions of the prayer. The "thou" petitions all have the word "thy," referring to God. They all have the verb in the third person singular. In the Greek text, they all begin with the verb. Finally, they are simply placed one after the other, without conjunctions. The "we" petitions differ in all four respects. They all have the words "us" or "our." They all have the verb in the second person singular. They all begin with some word other than the verb, and they are joined by conjunctions.

These comparisons between the two groups of petitions are based on the Greek text. Jesus originally gave the prayer in a Semitic language, either Hebrew or Aramaic, and scholars have made a number of attempts to reconstruct the original wording. Although these differ somewhat among themselves, it is interesting to notice that most of the differences between the "thou" petitions and the "we" petitions also appear in the Semitic reconstructions.[6] It is very likely, therefore, that the distinct division between the two sets of petitions was also characteristic of the Semitic form of the prayer as Jesus gave it.

Corresponding to the major sections of the Lord's Prayer, the next four chapters of this study will deal with the address to God, the "thou" petitions, the "we" petitions, and the doxology. Since the versions in Matthew and Luke both share this structure, apart from the doxology, this will be the most convenient way to treat both forms together. Before we turn to these sections of the Lord's Prayer, we may consider three further issues that sometimes arise in connection with the prayer: whether Jesus himself actually gave the prayer, what was its original form, and what was the original language.

The Authenticity of the Lord's Prayer

Scholars usually accept the view that Jesus himself gave the Lord's Prayer in one form or another. Occasionally, however, some interpreters have suggested that the early Christian community composed the prayer on the basis of certain sayings and teachings of Jesus. There are some fairly close parallels to the Lord's Prayer, for example, in Jesus' words in Gethsemane. As Mark records the incident, Jesus addressed God as "Abba, Father," and he prayed, "not what I will, but what thou wilt" (14:36). Shortly afterward he said to the disciples with him, "Watch and pray that you may not enter into temptation" (14:38). These words have some resemblance to the address of the Lord's Prayer and the petitions concerning God's will and the avoidance of temptation.

On the basis of this resemblance one interpreter has argued that Mark had no knowledge of the Lord's Prayer, and the early Christian community formulated the prayer from the account of Jesus' words in Gethsemane.[7] This type of argument, however, must assume what it tries to prove. The absence of the Lord's Prayer from Mark does not necessarily mean that Mark was unfamiliar with it. Nor does it necessarily mean that the early Christians composed the prayer later on the basis of materials in Mark. It is just as possible that Jesus gave the Lord's Prayer during the course of his ministry and then later, in Gethsemane, used somewhat similar phrases in his own prayer to God as these came to mind and were appropriate to the situation.

The strongest argument in favor of the authenticity of the Lord's Prayer is that parts of it, at least, satisfy the requirements of the *criterion of distinctiveness*. This is a method used by interpreters of the Gospels to identify those sayings and teachings of Jesus that have the greatest claim to authenticity. It does not necessarily identify all of the genuine words of Jesus, but it does help in recovering a basic core of material that may be regarded as genuine with a high degree of probability.[8]

According to the criterion of distinctiveness, a saying of Jesus may be regarded as authentic if it is distinctive in relation to the ideas and interests of Judaism and early Christianity. The saying must come from Jesus himself if it has no parallels in Judaism and if it does not reflect the outlook or beliefs of the early church. Such a saying would not have been created by the early Christians on the basis of their heritage in Judaism or their religious faith and practice as Christians.

In several respects the Lord's Prayer is distinctive in relation to Jewish prayers of the time. Jesus, for instance, probably used the Aramaic word *abba* in addressing God as "Father." This was a term characteristic of family life, and the Jews would have regarded it as too intimate and familiar to use in addressing God. Jesus spoke of the kingdom of God, as some Jewish prayers did, but he thought of the kingdom in a way that had no parallel in Judaism. Jesus made a connection between divine forgiveness and human forgiveness that apparently had no parallel in Jewish prayers of the time. He instructed his disciples to pray that they might receive "today" their "daily bread" or "bread for the morrow," and this particular petition again does not seem to have a parallel in Judaism. In these ways the Lord's Prayer reflects an understanding of God and his activity that differs from the outlook of ancient Judaism, and thus it bears the imprint of an original and creative mind.

In some ways the Lord's Prayer is also distinctive in relation to the ideas and interests of the early church. The early Christians formulated many beliefs about Jesus himself. They regarded him as Lord, Christ, and Savior. They proclaimed his death and Resurrection, and they believed that God had granted salvation and eternal life in him. In the final chapter of this study we will return to the question of the relationship between the Lord's Prayer and Christian faith. At this point it is important to notice that the prayer does not reflect any explicit Christian beliefs about Jesus himself. In this sense the Lord's Prayer is distinctive in relation to the outlook of the

early church. For this reason too, therefore, we may attribute
the prayer to Jesus himself.

The Original Form of the Lord's Prayer

If we believe that Jesus himself gave the Lord's Prayer, then
in what form did he give it? Was it in Luke's form, or Matthew's, or perhaps some earlier form from which both were
derived? Or did he give the prayer twice, in the forms now
represented by Luke and Matthew? These are the main possibilities with regard to the original form of the prayer. Although
we cannot reach a definite solution to this problem, we may
look at some of the issues that are involved.

A number of commentators have argued that Luke's form of
the prayer is more original than Matthew's. Three factors in
particular support this position. First, the early Christians cher-
ished the Lord's Prayer as the only prayer that they had received from Jesus himself. They would have been very reluctant
to remove anything from it. They might have added to it, if
they felt that Jesus had given the prayer as a brief model that
could receive additions or expansions. But they would not have
abridged a prayer that was as important as the Lord's Prayer.

A second consideration, closely related to the first, is the general principle that religious texts tend to get longer rather than
shorter as they are handed down and used within a community.
Luke has a short collection of Jesus' teachings, for example,
known as the Sermon on the Plain (6:20–49). Matthew has a
much longer collection of teachings called the Sermon on the
Mount (chaps. 5–7). The Sermon on the Plain probably represents an early form of the collection, which grew with the addition of other teachings until it acquired the dimensions represented by the Sermon on the Mount. In a similar way the Lord's
Prayer may have grown from a short form into a longer form.

A third argument in favor of the originality of Luke's form is
that the additional materials in Matthew have the effect of making the prayer more suitable for use in worship, either public or
private. Luke's form might have seemed rather brief and abrupt
for this purpose. The additional materials in Matthew appear at

the end of the major sections of the prayer—the address, the "thou" petitions, and the "we" petitions. They serve to round out and complete each part of the prayer, and in this way they make the whole prayer more appropriate for liturgical use. The fact that the prayer evidently grew in this way as the early Christians used it in worship is an indication that Luke's form must be closer to the original prayer that Jesus gave.

Considerations such as these have led many people to think that Luke's form of the Lord's Prayer is more original than Matthew's. The arguments are indeed persuasive. But a number of scholars, on the other hand, have taken the position that Matthew has preserved the more original form of the prayer. We may look at their arguments and then try to evaluate each one.[10]

A first argument is that Matthew records a saying of Jesus concerning wordiness in prayer: "And in praying do not heap up empty phrases as the Gentiles do; for they think that they will be heard for their many words" (6:7). Matthew records this saying just before he gives the Lord's Prayer itself. He would not contradict this principle by making additions to the Lord's Prayer. He must be giving the Lord's Prayer as Jesus gave it, or, at least, as he believes that Jesus gave it.

A second argument is that Matthew's version of the prayer has no superfluous phrases or clauses that could be left out. Each word makes its contribution to the meaning of the whole prayer. We pray to God as Father, knowing that he is close to us but is also transcendent and majestic in heaven. We pray for the hallowing of his name and the coming of his kingdom, knowing that these must be in accordance with his will. We pray that we may avoid temptation, recognizing that temptation involves everything that is evil. When we think of the prayer in this way, we see that all of the "additional" material in Matthew is essential to the meaning of the prayer.

A third argument for the authenticity of Matthew's version is that this form of the prayer is very carefully composed and arranged. According to Jean Carmignac, the address and the "thou" petitions form a group of five lines, and the "we" petitions form another group of five lines. Carmignac argues that this type of balanced structure is the essential feature of the poems of the Dead Sea Scrolls, and he believes that this could well be true for Palestinian poetry in general at the beginning of the Christian era.[11] The shorter form of the prayer in Luke lacks this stylistic feature, since it does not fall into sections of approximately the same length. The balanced poetic structure of Matthew's version must indicate that Jesus composed the prayer thoughtfully and carefully, knowing that its symmetrical form would make it more suitable for his followers to learn, preserve, and use in worship.

A fourth factor is that Matthew's version of the Lord's Prayer is much more "Jewish" in nature. It is closely related to the prayers used in the worship of the synagogue, and it reflects Jewish terminology and ways of thinking. The address "Our Father who art in heaven," for instance, appears in Jewish prayers. Matthew's use of the word "debts" reflects an Aramaic idiom, in which "debts" is used in the sense of "sins." Luke's version has changed the word to "sins," which would be more intelligible to non-Jewish people. In ways such as these Matthew's version has a more distinctly Jewish character than Luke's version. Since Jesus himself had grown up within Judaism and had become accustomed to its types of prayer, he must have given the Lord's Prayer as Matthew preserves it.

A fifth consideration is that the *Didache* gives the Lord's Prayer in almost the same form as Matthew. The author of the *Didache* was probably not copying directly from Matthew, but instead he was giving the prayer as it was used in his own day. His evidence indicates that Matthew's form of the prayer was generally accepted and used in the early church. The popularity of Matthew's version must reflect the belief that it was more authentic than Luke's.

A final argument in favor of Matthew's version is that Luke has a tendency to abbreviate by omitting details that he regards as superfluous. Carmignac points out, for example, that Luke has only four Beatitudes, whereas Matthew has nine (Luke 6:20–22; Matt. 5:3–11). In a similar way Luke has only one

account of the multiplication of the loaves and the fish, while
Matthew and Mark each have two (Luke 9:10–17; Matt.
14:13–21; 15:32–39; Mark 6:30–44; 8:1–10). Luke's sense of
economy in writing may have led him to abridge the Lord's
Prayer by shortening the address and omitting the final parts of
the "thou" petitions and the "we" petitions.

The cumulative force of these arguments requires that we
consider seriously the possibility that Matthew's form of the
Lord's Prayer is more original than Luke's. Matthew's version
came into general use at a very early time, and it has remained
popular up to the present day. The very fact that Matthew's
version has been so well known would perhaps make us wel-
come any evidence in favor of its authenticity. Later we shall
raise the question whether it makes any essential difference in
our understanding of the Lord's Prayer if Luke's version is actually closer to the original. But at this point we must examine
the arguments that have been put forth in favor of Matthew's
form of the prayer.

The first argument was that Jesus opposed wordiness in
prayer, and thus Matthew or the early Christians before him
would not have made additions to the Lord's Prayer. It is
doubtful, however, that this argument really applies to the
Lord's Prayer. The word translated "heap up empty phrases"
(Matt. 6:7) means literally to "babble." Jesus was probably
thinking of extremely long prayers, or else of magical incantations composed of nonsense syllables.[12] The Lord's Prayer does
not fit into these categories.

We must also remember that Jesus introduced the Lord's
Prayer, according to Matthew, with the instructions "Pray then
like this" (6:9). Jesus probably meant that the Lord's Prayer
was to be an example or model for prayer, rather than an un-
changeable formula. If this was the case, then the early Christians would not have felt that they were violating Jesus' understanding of the prayer by adding the few additional words that
we find in Matthew's version.

The second argument in favor of Matthew's version was that
it has no superfluous phrases or clauses that could be left out.

We shall consider this issue more fully in later chapters when we examine the meaning of the individual petitions. There is some reason to think, however, that the additional petitions in Matthew serve to explain more fully the meaning of the petitions that they follow. They bring out further aspects of the same ideas, but they do not introduce new ideas. In this sense the additional petitions in Matthew could be omitted without essentially changing the meaning of the prayer.

The third and fourth arguments concerned the poetic structure and Jewish nature of Matthew's version of the prayer. It is certainly true that Matthew's form has a more symmetrical poetic structure than Luke's. In some ways, at least, it is also more similar to Jewish prayers of the time. The problem is that arguments of this type can work both ways. They can suggest that Jesus himself gave the Lord's Prayer in Matthew's form. They can also suggest that early Christians of a Jewish background expanded the short form of the prayer to round out its poetic structure and make it more similar to Jewish prayers of the time. The early Christians would have regarded this as a legitimate procedure if they believed that Jesus gave the Lord's Prayer as a model for prayer rather than a fixed, invariable formula.

The fifth argument in favor of Matthew's version rested on the evidence of the *Didache*. It is true that the *Didache* gives a form of the prayer that is very similar to Matthew's. But the *Didache* probably came from the same general area in which the Gospel of Matthew had been written a generation or two earlier. It indicates that Matthew's form was prevalent in that area, but otherwise it does not tell us anything more than the Gospel of Matthew itself about the original form of the prayer as Jesus gave it.

The sixth argument in favor of Matthew's version was that Luke abridged the longer form of the prayer to eliminate phrases that he regarded as superfluous. It is true that Luke sometimes shows this sense of economy in writing. But his accounts of various incidents are not always shorter than those in Matthew and Mark. In a number of cases his accounts are at least as long as the corresponding passages in the other Gospels (e.g., Luke 6:6–11; 7:1–10, 18–23; 9:57–60). He might have been very reluctant to abridge the Lord's Prayer, since it was the only prayer that Jesus had given his followers. It is also difficult to understand why Luke would have omitted the petitions concerning God's will and deliverance from evil. Elsewhere in his Gospel he has only one reference to doing God's will (22:42) and only one possible reference to "evil" or "the evil one" (6:45). If he had known these petitions as part of the Lord's Prayer, he would certainly have recognized that they did not duplicate other passages in his Gospel.

In considering the question of the original form of the Lord's Prayer we have looked at various reasons for preferring either Luke's form or Matthew's. There are, of course, other ways of looking at the problem. Possibly Jesus gave the Lord's Prayer twice, in the forms now represented by Luke and Matthew.[13] Possibly he originally gave the prayer in a form that was different from both Luke and Matthew.[14] Possibly we cannot make any final decision on the relative authenticity of the versions in Luke and Matthew.[15] All of these views have been represented in recent scholarship, and they indicate that the question is still a matter of discussion.

If we ask whether Luke's version or Matthew's is closer to the original form of the prayer, the arguments in favor of Luke do seem to be more persuasive. There does not seem to be any adequate reason why Luke, or the early Christians before him, would want to abridge the Lord's Prayer. It is much more likely that Matthew, or the early Christians before him, expanded each section of the prayer to make it more suitable for use in worship and more similar in terminology and poetic structure to the Jewish prayers that they were familiar with.

This does not mean, of course, that the early Christians were trying to change the meaning of the prayer. They probably believed that Jesus had given the Lord's Prayer as a model for prayer that could receive some additions or expansions. But if this explanation is correct, it does suggest that Jesus probably gave the Lord's Prayer much as we now have it in Luke's version.

It is important to recall at this point that the forms of the prayer in Matthew and Luke both share the essential structure of address, "thou" petitions, and "we" petitions. In general, the additional material in Matthew's version brings out certain aspects of themes already present in the prayer, instead of introducing distinctly new ideas. For these reasons the two versions of the prayer are much more alike than it might seem at first sight. It does not alter our essential understanding of the prayer, therefore, if we take the view that Luke's version is probably closer to the form that Jesus gave.

The Language of the Lord's Prayer

The last problem that we will consider in this introductory chapter is the question of the language in which Jesus gave the Lord's Prayer. Here again we will find that scholarly opinion is not unanimous. But we need to examine the issue because in some instances our understanding of the meaning of a word in the Lord's Prayer is related to the question of the language in which Jesus originally gave the prayer.

As we saw previously, the earliest texts of the Lord's Prayer are given in Matthew, Luke, and the *Didache*. These come from the latter part of the first century and the early part of the second, and they are all written in Greek. It is virtually certain, however, that Jesus did not give the prayer in Greek. He might have known some Greek, since he lived most of his life in Galilee and could have had some contact with Greek-speaking people in Galilee and adjacent areas. But in general he carried out his ministry among the Jewish people. He would have given them the Lord's Prayer in a Semitic language, either Aramaic or Hebrew. Later, sometime before Matthew and Luke were written, the prayer was translated into Greek for the benefit of Greek-speaking Christians.

Hebrew was the language in which most of the Old Testament had been written. Aramaic was a related language in which a few later parts of the Old Testament were written.[16] Beginning as early as the Assyrian period, and continuing through the Babylonian, Persian, and Hellenistic periods, Aramaic served as the language of international diplomacy in the Near East. By the time of Jesus, Aramaic had evidently replaced Hebrew as the everyday spoken language in Palestine. Hebrew remained in use to some extent as a literary and liturgical language, although it is uncertain how widely it was understood by people in general.

Our problem is to determine whether Jesus would have given the Lord's Prayer in Aramaic or Hebrew. Many interpreters believe that he gave it in Aramaic, on the principle that this was the everyday spoken language. Recently, however, Jean Carmignac has argued that Hebrew was the more appropriate language for a formal, corporate prayer of this kind. He points out especially that the communal prayers of the Dead Sea Scrolls are in Hebrew, while only the private prayers of individual persons are recorded in Aramaic.[17] He believes that the ordinary people of Palestine could understand simple prayers in Hebrew, and he regards it as quite likely that Jesus gave the Lord's Prayer in Hebrew.[18]

One approach to this problem is to look at Jewish prayers that were used in Jesus' day. In particular we may consider the Eighteen Benedictions, the Morning Prayer, the Evening Prayer, and the Kaddish. These prayers all have parallels to various sections of the Lord's Prayer, and in their early forms they probably go back to Jesus' time. The texts of the first three have come down to us in Hebrew. The present text of the Kaddish is partly in Hebrew and partly in Aramaic, but the oldest parts are in Aramaic.[19] The fact that the first three are in Hebrew gives some support to the idea that ordinary people of the time did understand some Hebrew. We should also notice, however, that the Morning Prayer and the Evening Prayer are individual prayers, and the Kaddish is a corporate prayer. This weakens Carmignac's argument that Jesus would have regarded Hebrew as more appropriate for a corporate prayer like the Lord's Prayer. We cannot be certain, furthermore, that the

Eighteen Benedictions was always recited in Hebrew, for the Mishnah states that it could be said in any language.[20]

Jewish worship services in Jesus' day also used both Hebrew and Aramaic. The Shema, for example, was a confession of faith in the one God and his commandments.[21] It was originally in Hebrew, but it could be recited in any language.[22] Recitation of the Shema had an important place in the worship services of the synagogues and the Jerusalem temple.[23] The Eighteen Benedictions became an essential part of synagogue worship after the end of the first century, and it is possible that the prayer was already being used in the synagogue in Jesus' time. Certain parts of the Eighteen Benedictions (numbers 16, 17, 18, and perhaps 6) were also used in the worship of the temple. As we saw above, the Mishnah states that this prayer could be said in any language. The priestly or Aaronic blessing (Num. 6:24–26) was also used in both synagogue and temple worship. The Mishnah required that this blessing be spoken in Hebrew.[24]

Reading from Scripture was also a central feature of synagogue worship. The account in Luke 4:16–19 tells of an occasion on which Jesus himself did this. In Jesus' time the Scripture consisted of the Law and the Prophets. The Law was the Pentateuch, or the first five books of the Old Testament. The Prophets included the historical books (Joshua, Judges, 1 and 2 Samuel, 1 and 2 Kings) as well as the books of the various prophets (such as Hosea and Isaiah). The Law and the Prophets were both written in Hebrew. In the synagogue it was customary for someone to read selections from them in Hebrew, while an interpreter stood by to translate the words into Aramaic. The interpreter translated after every verse of the Law, because it was especially important, and after every three verses of the Prophets.

Since Hebrew was used to some extent in Jewish prayers and worship services, it is possible that the ordinary people of the time could have understood and learned the Lord's Prayer in Hebrew. It is likely, however, that they would have understood the prayer more easily in Aramaic. The fact that the Law and the Prophets were translated into Aramaic in the synagogue indicates that the common people felt more at home in this language. Throughout his ministry Jesus made a special effort to associate with the common people, and he drew most of his followers from them. In all likelihood, he would have given them the Lord's Prayer in the language that would be easiest for them to understand.

Another reason for thinking that Jesus gave the Lord's Prayer in Aramaic is that two words within the prayer itself seem to reflect a background that is Aramaic rather than Hebrew. The first of these is the word "father" in the address of the prayer. In his own prayers Jesus almost always addressed God as "Father." Usually, of course, the Gospels use the Greek word for father when they record Jesus' prayers. But Mark relates that Jesus' prayer in Gethsemane began with the words, "Abba, Father, all things are possible to thee" (14:36). This verse is especially important because it shows that Jesus used *abba*, the Aramaic word for father, in addressing God. It is very probable that *abba* underlies the Greek word for father in the other accounts of Jesus' prayers. Jesus was evidently accustomed to using this Aramaic term whenever he prayed to God as Father.[25]

Since Jesus used *abba* in his own prayers, it is very likely that he also used it to begin the prayer that he gave to his disciples.[26] The word *abba* could be used simply as a form of address, meaning "father." In this sense it evidently underlies Luke's version of the Lord's Prayer. In everyday speech *abba* was sometimes used rather freely to mean "our father," even though the suffix for "our" was not attached to it. In this sense it may underlie the address in Matthew's form of the Lord's Prayer.[27] Matthew's form may also reflect the influence of Jewish prayers, such as the Eighteen Benedictions and the *Ahaba Rabba* ("Great Love"), which addressed God with the Hebrew expression for "our father."

Two passages in Paul's letters confirm that the early Christian community used *abba* in addressing God. Paul wrote to the Galatians, "And because you are sons, God has sent the Spirit of his Son into our hearts, crying 'Abba! Father!' " (Gal. 4:6). In a similar way he wrote to the church at Rome, "When we cry, 'Abba! Father!' it is the Spirit himself bearing witness with our spirit that we are children of God" (Rom. 8:15–16). These quotations indicate that for some time, at least, the early Christians used the Aramaic word *abba* to address God as Father, even when Greek had become their predominant language. The most likely explanation for this usage is that Jesus himself had introduced the term by using it in the address of the Lord's Prayer.[28] The early Christians continued to use it as a distinctive way of expressing their new relationship to God.

A second term in the Lord's Prayer that points to an Aramaic background is the word "debts." In the petition for forgiveness, Matthew's version has the Greek word for debts, while Luke's version has the usual Greek word for sins. In this case it is clear that Matthew's version must reflect the original wording of the petition. The term "debts" was not ordinarily used in a religious sense in Greek. Luke, or the tradition on which he was dependent, substituted a more general term that was more intelligible to Greek-speaking Christians. Matthew evidently retained the word "debts" because its religious sense was sufficiently clear, even in Greek, for Christians of a Jewish background.

The term "debts" reflects a background that is Aramaic rather than Hebrew. The Aramaic word for debt, *choba*, became a common term in Judaism in the religious sense of "sin" or "guilt." It expressed the idea that men became debtors to God whenever they transgressed his law, so that they must try to remove their indebtedness by performing good deeds or asking for God's forgiveness.[29] This figurative use of the word "debt," however, was characteristic of Aramaic rather than Hebrew. The usual Hebrew terms for "debt" did not have the figurative sense of "sin," and the various terms for "sin" did not have the commercial or legal background of "debt."[30] The two ideas overlapped in Aramaic vocabulary but not in Hebrew.

These are the kinds of data that we must take into account when we ask whether Jesus gave the Lord's Prayer in Hebrew or Aramaic. The Jewish people would have been exposed to some

Hebrew in worship services, and they might have understood the Lord's Prayer in Hebrew. In all probability, however, they would have understood the prayer better in Aramaic. Since Jesus was especially interested in bringing his message to the common people, who used Aramaic as their everyday language, it is very likely that he gave them the Lord's Prayer in Aramaic.

Chapter Two

The Address

Our Father who art in heaven: Father:
        (Matt. 6:9)   (Luke 11:2)

In this chapter we will consider first the question whether Matthew's or Luke's form of the address is closer to the original prayer that Jesus gave. Then we will consider the various meanings that the term "Father" can have as a designation for God. In this connection we will look at a number of examples from the ancient Near East, the Greco-Roman world, the Old Testament, and Judaism. Finally, we will examine Jesus' use of the term "Father" in his various teachings and sayings. We will be especially concerned to delineate the distinctive meaning of the term *abba* as the address to God at the beginning of the Lord's Prayer.

The Address in Matthew and Luke

Matthew's form of the address is very familiar today. It has been the customary opening for the Lord's Prayer throughout Christian history, since Matthew's version of the entire prayer became popular at a very early time. The address in Matthew was understood to be a reverent, well-balanced liturgical expression that was especially appropriate for both public and private prayer.

In his other teachings, apart from the Lord's Prayer, it is possible that Jesus occasionally referred to God as the "Father in heaven" or "heavenly Father."[1] This usage would provide the main support for the view that Matthew's opening of the Lord's Prayer is original. In this connection we may notice that the phrase "Father in heaven" appears once in the Gospel of Mark: "And whenever you stand praying, forgive, if you have anything against any one; so that your Father also who is in

23

heaven may forgive you your trespasses" (11:25). In this way Mark, which was written earlier than Matthew, gives some support to the view that Jesus used the phrase "Father in heaven." We should notice, however, that this is the only occurrence of such a phrase in Mark. Since the verse in Mark is concerned with prayer and forgiveness, it may have been influenced by the use of the Lord's Prayer in the early church.

In contrast to Matthew's form of the address, Luke's form might appear rather brief and abrupt. Possibly the early Christians felt that the single word "Father" was less respectful or reverent as a way of addressing God. Yet in the preceding chapter we considered a number of reasons for thinking that Luke's form of the Lord's Prayer is generally closer to the original than Matthew's. In all probability this is the case with the address. In particular we may look at five factors suggesting that the brief address in Luke is more original than Matthew's form.

At first consideration is that the single word "Father" is the most accurate translation of the Aramaic term *abba*. As we saw earlier, Jesus almost always began his own prayers by addressing God as "Father." The only exception was his cry from the cross (Matt. 27:46; Mark 15:34), which was a quotation from Psalm 22:1. Jesus probably used the word *abba* in addressing God as Father, and he probably used it also when he gave the Lord's Prayer to his disciples. Luke reflects this usage accurately when he begins his version of the prayer with the Greek word for father.

A second factor is that there is no adequate reason to explain why Luke would want to abridge "Our Father who art in heaven" to "Father." We can readily understand, on the other hand, why Matthew or the early Christians before him would expand a brief address into a longer one. Because it was so full and well-rounded, the longer form would appear more appropriate for actual usage. It would also appeal to the liturgical sensitivity of Christians of a Jewish background, who were familiar with the rich heritage of prayer in Judaism.

A third factor concerns the usage of the Gospel writers. Apart from the Lord's Prayer, Matthew uses the expressions "Father in heaven" and "heavenly Father" much more often than the other Gospels. He uses them nineteen times, whereas Mark and Luke each use them only once.[2] It is possible that Matthew had access to special sources of Jesus' teachings that used these phrases. It is also possible, on the other hand, that Matthew or the tradition that he used was responsible for expanding a simple "Father" to "Father in heaven" or "heavenly Father."

There is some evidence, fourthly, that the phrase "Father in heaven" entered the theological vocabulary of Palestinian Judaism in the period A.D. 50–80. The earliest writer to use the phrase was apparently Johannan b. Zakkai, who taught during this period. Two sayings which are attributed to him use the expressions "their Father in heaven" and "our Father in heaven."[3] The phrase is also attributed to Zadok, about A.D. 70, in the following Jewish tradition:

Once R. Zadok went into the (destroyed) sanctuary. He said, "My Father, who art in heaven, thou hast destroyed thy city and burned thy temple, and remainest indifferent and silent." Immediately R. Zadok fell asleep. Then he saw how God stood in mourning, and the angels of the service mourned behind him. He said, "Have confidence, Jerusalem."[4]

It is significant that the phrase "Father in heaven" began to appear in Palestinian Judaism during the same decades in which the tradition of Jesus' teachings was being preserved and molded in Christian circles. It is quite possible that this Jewish usage influenced the development of Christian tradition. Matthew, in turn, drew upon such tradition when he wrote his Gospel about A.D. 85. In some instances, at least, this influence from Judaism may account for the relatively frequent occurrence of the phrase "Father in heaven" in Matthew.

A final consideration supporting the authenticity of Luke's form of address is that the phrases "Father" and "Father in heaven" do not have quite the same meaning. Although their meanings overlap to a considerable extent, each has a distinctive emphasis. If the brief address "Father" was expanded to "Father in heaven," then the special significance of the single word "Father" was in danger of being lost.

To examine this issue more closely, we may notice first that in his own prayers, as they are recorded in the first three Gospels, Jesus addressed God as "Father" rather than "Father who art in heaven" or "heavenly Father."[5] In all probability, as we have seen, he used the Aramaic term *abba* on these occasions. His prayers gave expression to several themes: his thankfulness to God,[6] his dedication to God's will,[7] his request for forgiveness for others,[8] and his complete trust in God's loving care.[9]

When Jesus used the Aramaic *abba* in these prayers, he employed a word that was drawn from home life. Little children used it to speak to their fathers, and grown-up sons continued to use it as a deferential form of address to their fathers. Because of its background in family life, no Jew of the time would have thought of using *abba* in addressing God. Jesus' use of the term reflected his awareness of his close relationship to God and his commitment to doing God's will.

If Jesus used the single word *abba* as the opening of the Lord's Prayer, then he was inviting the disciples to use the same term that he himself used in addressing God. He was giving them the privilege of entering into a new relationship with God that involved a new understanding of God's nature, activity, and will. In doing this he was establishing the nucleus of a new human community on earth that would be receptive and responsive to God's working in the world. Through his own unique relationship to God, Jesus was inviting the disciples to receive a new understanding of God and enter into a new relationship with God.

The meaning of the phrase "Father in heaven" overlapped to some extent with that of *abba*, "Father." It too, for example, could express the idea of confidence in God's love and mercy:

R. Eliezer (about A.D. 90) said, "On whom should we lean for support? On our Father who is in heaven."[10]

They ask for mercy before their Father in heaven.[11]

In a similar way the phrase "Father in heaven" could express the idea of dedication to God's will:

Judah b. Tema said, "Be bold as a leopard, swift as an eagle, fast as a stag, and strong as a lion, to do the will of thy Father who is in heaven."[12]

My people, children of Israel, as our Father is merciful in heaven, you should be merciful on earth.[13]

The meaning of "Father in heaven" corresponded to Jesus' use of the term *abba* in expressing confidence in God's care and dedication to his will. In Judaism, however, the phrase "Father in heaven" took on an additional function. In the period after the destruction of the Jerusalem temple in A.D. 70, it served to reassure the Jews of God's reality and his continuing care for them. It reminded them that God was still in heaven and was still concerned about the suffering or persecution that they were experiencing on earth.[14]

The story of Zadok's dream in the temple, quoted above, depicted the heavenly Father standing in mourning over the destruction of the temple. In this way it reassured the Jews that God was not indifferent to their plight. The following passage illustrates the similar idea that the heavenly Father is concerned about his people who are scattered throughout the world:

Our Father who art in heaven, show us mercy and love for thy great name's sake, which is named over us; and fulfill for us, O Lord our God, what is written, "At that time I will bring you home" (Zeph. 3:20).[15]

In this respect the phrase "Father in heaven" acquired a distinctive meaning of its own. The idea of God's continuing reality and care was very important, of course, to the Jewish people after the destruction of the temple. But the expression "Father in heaven" did not have the special significance of Jesus' term, *abba*. If Jesus instructed his disciples to address God by the same term that he himself used, then the distinctive meaning of this term was in danger of being lost by the expansion of "Father" to "Father in heaven." Only the term *abba*, "Father," conveyed the meaning of a new relationship with God, made possible through Jesus, and the beginning of a new community of disciples on earth.

These are the various factors that we must take into consideration when we try to decide whether Matthew's or Luke's form of address is closer to the original prayer that Jesus gave. It is possible that Jesus did use the expression "Father in heaven," as

Matthew indicates. It is very likely, however, that Luke's single word "Father" has accurately preserved an original *abba* at the beginning of the prayer.

God as Father in the Ancient Near East

Later in this chapter we will return to a further consideration of the term "Father" in Judaism and in Jesus' teachings. At this point we may broaden our inquiry by looking at the meaning of the word as a designation for God in the ancient Near East, the Greco-Roman world, and the Old Testament. This kind of survey will help us to understand further the distinctive way in which Jesus used the term.

The word "Father," when it is applied to God, may be used in three ways. It may indicate that God is the creator of the world and the ultimate source of human life. It may depict God as the sovereign ruler, who exercises authority over the world and requires obedience to his will. Or it may present God as helper and protector, who provides for men's welfare and gives them aid in time of need. Sometimes, of course, these functions may overlap. This is especially true of the second and third, for a particular action or law of God may express his sovereignty and at the same time promote human welfare. But the terms "creator," "ruler," and "helper" represent the primary ways in which God may be perceived when he is referred to as Father.

In ancient Egypt the sun-god, Amon-Re, was regarded as the father of the gods and the creator of everything that exists:

> Hail to thee, Amon-Re . . .
> The lord of truth and father of the gods,
> who made mankind and created the beasts . . .
> Maker of all mankind,
> Creator and maker of all that is.[16]

This hymn does not speak directly of Amon-Re as the father of men in general. In Egyptian thought the pharaoh was regarded as the son of god, the living representation of the divine on earth. For this reason the references to deity as the father of men are almost always limited in scope to the pharaoh himself. Often these references express the thought that the god, as father, watches over and protects the pharaoh—e.g., "His father Amon-Re was the magical protection of his person, guarding the Ruler."[17]

The prayer of Rameses II expresses the similar idea that the god Amon comes to the pharaoh's aid and vanquishes his enemies:

What then, O my Father Amon? Does a father forget his son? I call upon thee, O my Father Amon, I am in the midst of enemies without number whom I do not recognize. . . . And I found that Amon had come, because I had called him. He gives me his hand; he is with me; I am filled with joy. . . . My Father Amon, accompanying me, destroyed the nations like straw before me.[18]

This prayer reflects a sense of complete trust in the deity and reliance on his guidance and help. We should notice, however, that this relationship exists only between the god and the pharaoh, without extending to men in general. We should also notice that the god's protection takes the form of granting victory in military affairs. The occasional references in Egyptian writings to the times when the pharaoh carries out the "commands" of his god also refer to this type of activity.[19]

It appears that only the pharaoh in ancient Egypt could speak of his god as Father. W. Marchel, however, has called attention to the recent study of scarabs, which has provided new information about religious ideas among the Egyptian people. These scarabs were small carvings of beetles, which the ancient Egyptians regarded as sacred. One of the scarabs bears the inscription, "God is my Father," suggesting that ordinary people too could place a warm personal trust in their god.[20]

If we turn to ancient Mesopotamia, we see even more clearly that a god could be addressed as Father in the sense of creator, ruler, and helper. All three functions are combined in the following hymn to the moon-god, who is addressed here primarily by his Sumerian name, Nanna:

O Lord, hero of the gods, who in heaven and earth is exalted in his
   uniqueness,
Father Nanna, lord Anshar, hero of the gods . . .
Begetter, merciful in his disposing, who holds in his hand the life of the
   whole land . . .

O father begetter of gods and men, who founds shrines and establishes offerings . . .
Father begetter, who looks favorably upon all living creatures . . .
O Lord, decider of the destinies of heaven and earth, whose word no one alters . . .
Thou! Thy word causes truth and justice to be, so that the people speak the truth.[21]

The moon-god is also referred to as "Father" in other writings from ancient Mesopotamia.[22] Sometimes other gods receive this designation as well. The sun-god Shamash, for instance, is described as "the judge of truth, the father of the fatherless."[23] Marduk, the god of Babylon, was called "Merciful Father."[24] Most of these examples depict the god as the divine helper who gives men his protection and care.

God as Father in the Greco-Roman World

In the Greco-Roman world it was also rather common to refer to a god or address him as "Father." The exact meaning of this term depended on the writer and also, to some extent, his period of time. In early Greek literature, for example, Homer frequently referred to Zeus as "Father of gods and men."[25] He did not mean that Zeus was the creator of mankind, but he was depicting Zeus as the supreme ruler over heaven and earth who administered the affairs of both gods and men.

Homer also represents men calling on Zeus in prayer and addressing him as "Father Zeus." In Greek this is *Zeu pater*, from which the Latin word Jupiter is derived. Such prayers express the hope that Zeus, as Father, will grant his aid or protection. At the same time they often reflect the recognition that Zeus is the divine ruler and his will is supreme. The following prayer, in which the Greeks and the Trojans joined on one occasion early in the Trojan war, combines these two meanings of the term "Father":

Father Zeus, that rulest from Ida, most glorious, most great, whichsoever of the twain it be that brought these troubles upon both peoples, grant that he may die and enter the house of Hades, whereas to us there may come friendship and oaths of faith.[26]

From the time of Homer up to the threshold of the Christian era, a number of Greek writers addressed Zeus as "Father." The prayers that they record continue to depict him in the roles of ruler and helper, with emphasis on the thought that he is the Father who answers prayer and helps men in time of need. The following prayer from Euripides expresses a warm sense of personal trust in Zeus and confidence in the value of his help:

> Zeus, Father art thou called, and the Wise God:
> Look upon us, and from our woes redeem;
> And, as we drag our fortunes up the steep,
> Lay to thine hand: a finger-touch from thee,
> and good-speed's haven long-desired we win.[27]

In Greek thought the view of Zeus as Father in the sense of ruler and helper is attested from a very early period. It was apparently somewhat later, however, that Zeus or other divinities were called Father in the sense of creator. In the philosophical terminology of the *Republic*, Plato spoke of the idea of the good as "the father."[28] He regarded this idea as "the cause for all things of all that is right and beautiful, giving birth in the visible world to light and the source of light, and being itself in the intelligible world the source of truth and reason."[29]

Later, in the creation myth of the *Timaeus*, Plato spoke of the creator-god, the demiurge, as "maker and father of all."[30] Plato did not necessarily identify the idea of the good and the demiurge, for they served different functions in their respective contexts. But both concepts, especially that of the demiurge, influenced the later development of Greek thought.

In his famous hymn to Zeus, the Stoic philosopher Cleanthes depicts Zeus as creator, ruler, and helper. Near the beginning of his prayer he indicates that Zeus is the ultimate ground of human existence: "For we are thy offspring" (v. 4). Later he prays that Zeus will help men and give them an understanding of the principles by which he rules the world:

Deliver men from their dark ignorance; drive it away, O Father, far from their soul, and grant that they may attain the thought that guides thee in governing everything with justice.[31]

In a similar way a later Stoic, Epictetus, speaks of Zeus as Father in the sense of creator, ruler, and helper. Zeus is the creator of mankind, the ruler over the universe, and the helper who gives men strength in meeting adversity.[32] Epictetus gives special emphasis to the thought that the fatherhood of Zeus has certain consequences for the understanding of human nature and conduct. If a man is aware of his divine origin, and if he knows that he has a part of the divine reality within him, he will do nothing unworthy of his own nature or his divine father.[33]

As a final example of the use of "Father" in the Greco-Roman world, we may look at the group of religious cults that are known as mystery religions. These cults originated in various parts of the Roman Empire, such as Egypt and the Near East, but they spread throughout the empire and won many adherents in the late pre-Christian and early Christian periods. The term "Father" as a form of address for the deity was frequent in the mystery religions. It was used, for example, of Attis, Osiris, Mithras, and Helios (Sun). The main emphasis in these cults was that the initiates received the promise of personal immortality by sharing in the divinity's power over death. In this sense they were "reborn," so that they became "sons" of their divine "Father."[34]

We have been looking at the use of the word "Father" for God in the ancient Near East and the Greco-Roman world. Our survey has not been complete, for we have not examined all the cultures within these areas or considered other parts of the ancient world. But it will be helpful at this point to summarize our findings before we go on to examine the use of the word in the Old Testament and Judaism.

In the ancient Near East and the Greco-Roman world we found a number of examples in which a god is depicted as Father in the sense of creator, ruler, or helper. In particular, we noticed a number of examples of a warm sense of individual trust in the divine "Father" and reliance on his help. It is also important to notice that the term "Father" was applied to a god within the general context of polytheism. Addressing a god as

"Father" did not necessarily imply that he was the only god in existence or even that he was the only god who could be addressed in this way.

These general findings indicate that the use of the term "Father" was widespread in the ancient world. Many people used it, in a variety of ways, to designate or address their gods. Gottlob Schrenk has summarized the situation in this way: "Invocation of deity under the name of father is one of the basic phenomena of religious history. It is found among both primitive and culturally elevated peoples, both around the Mediterranean and in Assyria and Babylonia."[35]

The Question of Religious Truth

Christians today may raise the question of religious truth in relation to this widespread use of the word "Father" in the ancient world. It is a central part of Christian faith to believe that there is only one God, who made himself known in a unique way in Jesus Christ. From this standpoint Christians may ask whether the use of the term "Father" in the ancient world can reflect a genuine knowledge of God. Although it lies beyond the scope of this book to discuss this problem in detail, we can look at several solutions that have been offered in the past.

We may notice first that ancient Judaism faced a similar question in the pre-Christian period. The Jews believed that they had received a special knowledge of God, for he had chosen them as his covenant people and had given them his law through Moses. They held different views on the question of genuine spiritual truth and values in non-Jewish cultures. In the second century B.C., for example, the author of the Book of Jubilees argued that non-Jews could have no true knowledge of God. Since they had not received God's law, they could not hope to live according to his will or obtain salvation in the life to come.[36]

Another writing from the same period, the Testaments of the Twelve Patriarchs, reflected a more positive view toward non-Jewish peoples. According to this view, the law was given to enlighten every man, the task of the Jews was to bring God's salvation to all peoples, and the Jews themselves would be judged according to the best standards of conduct among non-Jewish peoples.[37] This writing suggested, at least, that non-Jews could have some genuine appreciation of religious truth and values.

In a similar way, early Christian writers took different positions on the question of religious truth in the various non-Christian religions and philosophies of the ancient world. A writer of the second century, Tertullian, represented an extremely negative evaluation of non-Christian thought. "What indeed," he wrote, "has Athens to do with Jerusalem?"[38] Even the finest of Greek philosophy, he felt, really had nothing in common with Christian faith. The insights and values of non-Christian thought were misleading and deceptive, since they had no relationship to God's revelation of himself in Jesus Christ.

Another Christian of the second century, Justin Martyr, developed a much more positive view toward other types of thought. He believed that the divine "Word" or "Logos" formed a bridge between non-Christian thought and Christian faith. Although the Logos appeared in its fullness only in Christ, a "seed" of the Logos was placed in the mind of every man long before Christ. In this sense those who lived according to the Logos could even be called Christians:

> We have been taught that Christ is the firstborn of God, and we have declared that he is the Logos, of whom every race of man were partakers, and those who lived according to the Logos are Christians, even though they have been thought atheists, as among the Greeks, Socrates and Heraclitus, and men like them.[39]

In one form or another this problem has occupied Christian thinkers up to the present day. In our present study we encounter the problem when we see that many people in the ancient world used the term "Father" to speak of their gods. They did not, of course, all use the word in the same way. The Egyptian pharaoh gave meanings and connotations to the term that were very different from those of the Stoic philosopher Cleanthes or the worshipers in the mystery religions. Nor, in general, did they attempt to use the word "Father" within a context of monotheism. In this sense alone their usage differs from the understanding of God in Judaism and Christianity.

Christian faith is based on the belief that God revealed himself most fully in Jesus Christ. Even Justin Martyr, sympathetic as he was to other types of thought, held to this belief. From this standpoint it would not be possible to say that the people of the ancient world had a full knowledge of God when they used the term "Father." It is possible, on the other hand, that in many instances they were making a genuine attempt to understand divine reality and express religious truth as they were able to perceive it. This is one approach, at any rate, by which a Christian today can recognize the uniqueness of his own heritage and at the same time appreciate the values and insights of the cultures of the ancient world.

God as Father in the Old Testament

We have given some attention to the question of assessing the religious "truth" of the non-Christian use of the word "Father" because it illustrates the kind of problem that arises whenever persons standing within a particular religious tradition try to evaluate the ideas and beliefs of other cultures and faiths. We may turn now to the Old Testament and ask how the ancient Israelites conceived of God as Father. We will continue to look for references to God as Father in the sense of creator, ruler, or helper. At the same time we will look for any distinctive ways in which the Israelites used the term. Since the Old Testament has relatively few direct references to God as Father, we will occasionally look at other passages that speak of Israel as the "son" of God or compare God's actions to those of a human father.[40]

The ancient Israelites believed that God was the creator of the world and everything in it. They expressed this belief in the first chapter of Genesis and also in a number of other passages of the Old Testament, such as Ps. 74, Ps. 136, and Isa. 40–55. But they were very reluctant to speak of God as Father in connection with his role as creator of the world. They thought of God

primarily as the Father of his covenant people Israel, and they
believed that he had become their Father in a special sense
when he delivered them from slavery in Egypt and led them
through the wilderness to their homeland. This covenant relationship with Israel is the background for a passage such as
Deut. 32:6, which speaks of God as Father in the sense of
"creator":

> Do you thus requite the Lord,
>   you foolish and senseless people?
> Is not he your father, who created you,
>   who made you and established you?

The verses that follow this passage indicate that the writer is
thinking of "creation" in the sense of God's decisive intervention in history on behalf of his people:

> For the Lord's portion is his people,
>   Jacob his allotted heritage.
> He found him in a desert land,
>   and in the howling waste of the wilderness;
> he encircled him, he cared for him,
>   he kept him as the apple of his eye . . .
> the Lord alone did lead him,
>   and there was no foreign god with him . . .
> then he forsook God who made him,
>   and scoffed at the Rock of his salvation.
>   (Deut. 32:9–10, 12, 15b)

These verses illustrate several meanings of the term "Father"
in a way that is typical of Old Testament thought. As Father,
God "created" Israel by making her his covenant people and
giving her a special purpose and identity. As Father, he was also
the helper and redeemer who protected and guided the people
in their wanderings. As Father, too, he was the ruler who expected the people to acknowledge him as their only God. But
after Israel left the wilderness and settled in the land of Canaan,
she became a "foolish and senseless people" who gave her loyalty
to other gods.

There are only a few other passages in the Old Testament
that speak of God as "Father" in the sense of "creator." Here
again God appears specifically as the Father of his people Israel:

> Yet, O Lord, thou art our Father;
>   we are the clay, and thou art our potter;
>   we are all the work of thy hand.
> Be not exceedingly angry, O Lord,
>   and remember not iniquity for ever.
> Behold, consider, we are all thy people.
>
>   (Isa. 64:8–9)

Have we not all one father? Has not one God created us? Why then are we faithless to one another, profaning the covenant of our fathers?

                               (Mal. 2:10)

The passage from Isaiah is a plea that God will be merciful and gracious to his people, because he created them for a purpose and can still intervene on their behalf. The passage from Malachi reminds the people that they should be faithful and righteous in their actions, since the God of the covenant is their Father. Each passage refers, in its own way, to the theme of creation, but each one understands God's fatherhood as an expression of his relationship to his people Israel.

The Old Testament prophets depict God as Father in the sense that he was the redeemer and ruler who delivered the people from Egypt and expected that they would respond to him with exclusive covenant loyalty. But the prophets also point out that Israel has shown constant ingratitude by worshiping other gods, refusing to acknowledge their own divine Father, and practicing evil in their lives:

> When Israel was a child, I loved him,
>   and out of Egypt I called my son.
> The more I called them,
>   the more they went from me;
> they kept sacrificing to the Baals,
>   and burning incense to idols.
>
>   (Hos. 11:1–2)

> Sons have I reared and brought up
>   but they have rebelled against me.
> The ox knows its owner,
>   and the ass its master's crib;
> but Israel does not know,
>   my people does not understand.
>
>   (Isa. 1:2a–3)

> Have you not just now called to me,
> "My father, thou art the friend of my youth—
> will he be angry for ever,
> will he be indignant to the end?"
> Behold, you have spoken,
> but you have done all the evil that you could.
>
> (Jer. 3:4–5)

Hosea, Isaiah, and Jeremiah all speak of God as Father in the sense that he helped Israel in the past and expects their response of obedience and faithfulness. But all feel compelled to add that Israel has been ungrateful and disobedient. If she is to continue as God's covenant people, she must trust in his renewed mercy rather than rely on her own righteousness. Like the other Old Testament quotations that we have examined, these passages understand God's fatherhood as an expression of his relationship to his covenant people.

It will be helpful at this point to summarize the main characteristics of the term "Father" as it is applied to God in the Old Testament. At the same time we may compare the Old Testament view with that of the various religions and cultures that we examined from the ancient Near East and the Greco-Roman world. Then we may look at some further aspects of the term which are less characteristic of the Old Testament as a whole and which come, in some instances, from the latter part of the Old Testament period.

In the Old Testament, God is depicted as Father in the sense of creator, ruler, and helper. In this general sense the Old Testament examples are parallel to those that we examined earlier from other cultures. But in four ways, at least, it would appear that Old Testament usage was quite distinctive in comparison to the other religions and cultures of the ancient world.

A first distinctive feature of Old Testament thought is that it depicts God as Father with special reference to his working in history on behalf of his covenant people Israel. God was the Father of Israel in the sense that he delivered her from slavery in Egypt, nurtured her in the desert, and guided her into her homeland. Even when the Old Testament writers depict God as

Father in the sense of "creator," their primary thought is that God "created" Israel through his activity in history.

This understanding of God as the Father who works in history is generally absent from the other cultures of the ancient Near East and the Greco-Roman world. It is true that people in these cultures often called on their gods to help them in specific situations. But we do not seem to meet the idea that God works throughout a period of many generations and centuries to guide, protect, and discipline a people with whom he stands in close covenant relationship.

A second characteristic of Old Testament usage, closely related to the first, is that God is primarily the Father of the people Israel. The Old Testament does not stress the idea that he is the Father of all men. It depicts God as the creator of all men, but it uses the term "Father" primarily as a way of indicating his relationship to his covenant people. In a similar way the Old Testament does not often use the term "Father" to express God's relationship to individual Israelites. He is primarily the Father of the people, and individual persons within Israel experience his fatherly guidance and care through his actions on behalf of the people as a whole.

In the other religions of the ancient world there is a partial parallel to this Old Testament viewpoint in the sense that gods are often depicted as national gods. But there is also a tendency to universalize and individualize the conception of divine fatherhood, so that a god may be represented as the father of all men or the father of individual persons. Old Testament thought lays primary emphasis on the corporate idea that God is the Father of his people Israel.

A third distinctive aspect of the Old Testament understanding of God as Father is that he is a moral God who expects his covenant people to respond to him with faithfulness and righteousness. Again and again, as we have seen in the passages quoted above, the Old Testament writers contrast God's fatherly care with the ingratitude and disobedience of the people. They stress that if Israel is to have any hope of continuing as

God's covenant people, she must trust in his renewed mercy and forgiveness rather than rely on her own righteousness.

The other religions and cultures of the ancient world do not seem to express this sharp contrast between the moral nature of a god and the people's failure to live in the ways that their god desires. Occasionally we find the thought that a god is the source of truth and justice, and we also find the similar idea that a man will do nothing unworthy of his divine father. But the continual contrast between the ethical requirements of God and the people's failure to obey would appear to be distinctive of the Old Testament's understanding of God as Father.

A fourth major feature of the Old Testament view is that the idea of God as Father is set within the context of monotheism. In the earlier Old Testament period this meant that the people were expected to worship God alone, with no other gods beside him (cf. Exod. 20:3). At some later point the idea of monotheism came to mean that God alone exists, that no other gods exist at all (cf. Isa. 44:6; 45:5). In either case the Old Testament understanding of God was distinctive. There does not seem to be any suggestion in other religions of the ancient world that divine fatherhood was restricted to the context of monotheism. To address a god as Father did not imply that this god alone should be worshiped or that he alone existed.

These four features are especially characteristic of the Old Testament view of God as Father. At the same time, they are distinctive in relation to other views in the ancient world. We should also notice that there are several further aspects of the Old Testament usage. We may look at these briefly, even though they are less characteristic of the Old Testament as a whole.

One of these further aspects is that God is occasionally described as the Father of the king of Israel.[41] God has a special relationship to the king in the sense that he establishes and maintains the Davidic throne in Jerusalem. The king becomes a special representative of the people before God, and he is also a channel through which God's care and protection flow outward to the people. God is the Father of the king, however, only in a figurative sense. There is probably no reason to think that the Israelite king was regarded, like the pharaoh in Egypt, as an incarnation of the deity.

Another idea that we occasionally find in the Old Testament is that God is the Father of the "righteous" Israelites, or "those who fear him." This idea appears in only a few Old Testament passages, and the majority of these, at least, are rather late in the Old Testament period.[42] This restriction of God's fatherhood rests on the belief that only those persons within Israel who respected God and served him faithfully could think of him as their Father.

In the Old Testament we also find occasional traces of the view that God is the Father of other peoples besides Israel. God is the Father of Israel in a special way, but he also has other "sons" to whom he has allotted portions of the earth.[43] From a rather early time in the Old Testament period, about the middle of the tenth century B.C., we encounter the view that God is creator of the world and sovereign over the various peoples of the earth.[44] The prophets of the eighth to sixth centuries B.C. also express the belief that God works through the histories of other nations. It is rare, however, for the Old Testament writers to use the specific word "Father" when they speak of God's relationship to the peoples and nations other than Israel.

In a few passages of the Old Testament we encounter the belief that God, as Father, will act in the future to restore the people from exile or help them in other ways to relieve their suffering. A passage in Jeremiah, for instance, illustrates vividly how the belief in God's fatherly care undergirds the expectation for deliverance from exile:

> With weeping they shall come,
>   and with consolations I will lead them back,
> I will make them walk by brooks of water,
>   in a straight path in which they shall not stumble;
> for I am a father to Israel,
>   and Ephraim is my first-born.
>
> (Jer. 31:9) [45]

The passages that reflect this belief tend to come from the latter parts of the Old Testament period. The idea differs from the usual Old Testament view, for it associates God's father-hood with deliverance in the future rather than the past. In our present study this belief is important, however, because it anticipates the structure of thought that we find in the Lord's Prayer. Jesus also lived at a time when the Jewish people were looking forward to some new action of God on their behalf. It is significant that in the Lord's Prayer the opening address, "Father," is followed immediately by the "thou" petitions, which ask God to intervene in history by hallowing his name and establishing his kingdom.

We have been looking at the major characteristics of the Old Testament use of "Father" with reference to God, and we have also examined several further aspects which are less prominent in the Old Testament as a whole. Before we leave our examination of the Old Testament, we may notice a surprising point about its use of this term. There does not seem to be a single prayer in the Old Testament in which God is actually addressed as "Father." Several times we find the statements, "Thou art our Father" (Isa. 63:16; 64:8) and "Thou art my Father" (Ps. 89:26; Jer. 3:4). Strictly speaking, however, these are probably statements rather than forms of direct address to God.[46]

Undoubtedly the ancient Israelites prayed to God with a genuine sense of trust in his care and commitment to his will. But they were extremely reluctant to address God as "Father." The reason may have been that they wished to avoid any suggestion that God was the mythical forefather or progenitor of the people. They believed that they had become the covenant people through God's intervention in history, rather than by way of descent from a mythical divine forefather.[47] The reluctance of the ancient Israelites to use the word "Father" in addressing God may partially explain the fact that this usage was still rare in the Palestinian Judaism of Jesus' day.

God as Father in Judaism

At the beginning of this chapter we looked at the meaning of the expression "Father in heaven," as it came into use in Judaism in the latter part of the first century A.D. We saw that this phrase expressed confidence in God's love and mercy, and dedication to doing his will. We also saw that after the destruction of the Jerusalem temple in A.D. 70 this phrase took on the specific function of reassuring the Jewish people of God's continuing presence and care.

At this point we may look more generally at the Jewish use of "Father" for God. We will be especially concerned with the question whether Jewish usage differed in any way from earlier Old Testament usage. As far as possible, we will limit our attention to Palestinian Judaism, since this was the religious environment within which Jesus formulated his own ideas and beliefs.

Beginning about 200 B.C., and continuing for several centuries, a number of Jewish authors produced the writings that are included in the collections known as the Apocrypha and the Pseudepigrapha. Many of these books come from outside of Palestine, and thus they fall outside the scope of our study.[48] In the writings of Palestinian origin, the word "Father" occurs very rarely as a designation for God. We do, however, find the following occurrences:

(And the Lord said unto Moses:) And their souls will cleave to Me and to all My commandments, and they will fulfill My commandments, and I will be their Father and they shall be My children. And they all shall be called children of the living God, and every angel and every spirit shall know, yea, they shall know that these are My children, and that I am their Father in uprightness and righteousness, and that I love them . . . And the Lord will appear to the eyes of all, and all shall know that I am the God of Israel and the Father of all the children of Jacob, and King on Mount Zion for all eternity.

(Bk. Jub. 1:24–25, 28; cf. 19:29)[49]

Yea, I cried: "O Lord, my Father art Thou,
For Thou art the hero of my salvation;
Forsake me not in the day of trouble,
In the day of wasteness and desolation."
(Sirach 51:10)[50]

Since the books of Jubilees and Sirach were written in the second century B.C., they are important as sources for understanding Judaism as it developed before the time of Jesus. In several ways they reflect ideas that are more characteristic of Judaism than the Old Testament. Both passages, for example, are oriented toward the future in their understanding of God's role as Father. The Old Testament expresses this idea only in a few passages, which tend to be relatively late.

The passage from Jubilees depicts God as the Father of all the people of Israel. At the same time, however, it implies that only those who follow his commandments can truly regard him as their Father. This tendency to restrict the scope of God's fatherhood is present in the Old Testament, as a relatively minor theme, but it becomes more prominent in Judaism.

In a similar way the passage from Sirach depicts God as the Father of the individual person; the person can then speak of God as "my Father." The individual person, of course, is still speaking as a member of the Jewish people. But the use of the word "Father" in this passage represents a tendency to individualize or personalize the idea of God's fatherhood, and in this sense it differs from the corporate conception that is predominant in the Old Testament.

We may notice also that the passage from Jubilees describes God as "Father . . . and King." The two ideas are not inconsistent since God's sovereignty is often an important aspect of his fatherhood. But the explicit connection of the two terms is noteworthy. Two Jewish prayers of the first century addressed God as "Our Father, our King," and in the Lord's Prayer itself the address "Father" is followed shortly by the petition that God may establish his kingdom.

Prayers are a very important source for the religious ideas and living faith of a people. We cannot always be certain exactly which Jewish prayers, or which parts of the prayers, go back to the time of Jesus. But two prayers which address God as "Father" were evidently in use in Jesus' day. The first is the *Ahaba Rabba*, or "Great Love." It formed part of the morning worship in the Jerusalem temple, and it was also used in the morning worship of the synagogue. The prayer began as follows:

With great love hast thou loved us, O Lord, our God, with great and exceedingly great forbearance hast thou ruled over us. Our Father, our

King, for the sake of our fathers who trusted in thee and whom thou taughtest the statutes of life, be gracious also to us and teach us. Our Father, merciful Father, have pity upon us and inspire us to perceive and understand, learn and teach, observe and do and keep and love all the words of the teaching of thy law.[51]

The second prayer is the Litany for the New Year. Its beginning and end, as quoted by R. Akiba, were as follows:

> Our Father, our King,
>   we have no other king but thee;
> our Father, our King,
>   for thine own sake have mercy upon us.[52]

Both of these prayers address God as "our Father, our King." The *Ahaba Rabba* depicts God as ruler and helper, and at the same time it illustrates how closely these two roles were interrelated in Jewish thinking about God. It suggests that the Father exercises his sovereignty in love, just as his love can take the form of teaching the people to obey his law. The beginning of the Litany for the New Year expresses the belief in monotheism. This was a central belief for the Jews of Jesus' time, just as it had been for the Israelites of the Old Testament period.

These seem to be the only two Jewish prayers from Palestine which address God as "Father" which can be traced back, with some degree of certainty, to Jesus' own time.[53] The Jewish people evidently did not make a common practice of addressing God as "Father." It is all the more significant, therefore, that Jesus customarily addressed God in this way and instructed his followers to do so when he gave them the Lord's Prayer.

The Jewish rabbis of the early Christian period continued to speak of God as Father in the sense of the ruler who expects men to obey his will, and also as the helper who shows mercy to his children and strengthens them in times of adversity. Earlier in this chapter, when we examined the phrase "Father in heaven," we looked at a number of passages illustrating these two ideas. The following passages also express the thought that the Jews are obligated to obey the will of their heavenly Father:

(God said,) "Although all are the work of my hands, I will reveal myself as Father and Maker only to those who do my will."[54]

R. Eleazar b. Jose (about A.D. 180) said, "All good deeds and works of love which the Israelites have practised in this world are great peace (makers) and great advocates between them and their heavenly Father."[55]

This emphasis on obeying God's will is closely related to the tendency in Judaism to restrict the idea of God's fatherhood to the righteous who demonstrate that they are worthy of being his children. Yet the Jews also emphasized that God was the source of mercy and forgiveness:

Thou art he whose mercy towards us is greater than that of a father towards his sons.[56]

R. Akiba (about A.D. 130) said, "Happy are you Israelites! Before whom are you purified, and who purifies you? Your Father in heaven."[57]

Like the writers of the Old Testament, the Jews of Jesus' time spoke of God as Father in the sense of ruler and helper, but seldom in the sense of creator. Like the Old Testament writers, they also thought of God primarily as the Father of the people or the community. But within this general conception they were more inclined to speak of God as the Father of the individual person, or the Father of the righteous who obeyed his law. They also used the word "Father" in addressing God in prayer, although, as we have seen, this usage was not extensive.

God as Father in the Teachings of Jesus

We may turn now to the question how Jesus used the word "Father" as a way of speaking about God or addressing God in prayer. We will ask especially how often he used the word, how he understood it, and how his usage may be compared to that of Judaism. A consideration of these issues will help us understand more clearly what Jesus meant when he began the Lord's Prayer by addressing God as "Father."

At the beginning of this chapter we noticed that the Gospel of Matthew uses the expressions "Father in heaven" and "heavenly Father" much more often than Mark and Luke. We also noticed that this type of phrase began to appear in Palestinian Jewish writings in the latter part of the first century A.D.

This was the period when the Christian traditions were being formulated which Matthew then incorporated in his Gospel.

In many instances, it is possible that Matthew reflects the influence of current Jewish usage or Palestinian Christian usage when he attributes these phrases to Jesus. We must be cautious, therefore, about using Matthew as a source for assuming that Jesus frequently referred to God as the "Father in heaven" or "heavenly Father." This is especially the case when parallel passages in the other Gospels fail to support Matthew's usage.

We face a similar problem when we ask how often Jesus referred to God simply as "Father." We find four instances in Mark, fifteen in Luke, and forty-two in Matthew.[58] Here again we must ask whether Matthew has reported Jesus' words accurately. The question is important, since Mark and Luke suggest that Jesus used the word "Father" with considerable restraint. Matthew, in contrast, indicates that he used it quite often.

We can approach this question from a slightly different direction if we ask what the various sources of the synoptic Gospels indicate about Jesus' use of the word "Father" with reference to God. Many interpreters of the New Testament believe that the Gospel of Mark was written first and that Matthew and Luke each used Mark as a source when they wrote their accounts of Jesus' ministry. In a similar way Matthew and Luke each employed a collection of Jesus' sayings that was evidently unknown to Mark. In addition, Matthew and Luke each had further sources of information, and each probably made occasional changes in the sources that he utilized.

From this standpoint, we can list the passages in which Jesus is reported to have used the word "Father" with reference to God:

> Mark—four instances[59]
> common to Matthew and Luke—eight instances[60]
> Luke alone—five instances[61]
> Matthew alone—thirty instances[62]

Here again we notice the much greater number of occurrences in Matthew. Some of these represent passages that occur only in Matthew, and we cannot compare them with the other Gospels. In a number of cases, however, Matthew uses the word "Father" when parallel passages in Luke or Mark have some other word. According to Matt. 6:26, for example, Jesus said, "Look at the birds of the air: they neither sow nor reap nor gather into barns, and yet your heavenly Father feeds them." The parallel verse in Luke 12:24 has the wording, "and yet God feeds them." According to Matt. 12:50, Jesus stressed the importance of doing "the will of my Father in heaven." The parallel verses in Mark 3:35 and Luke 8:21, however, have "God" instead of "Father in heaven."

In cases like this, it is very likely that Matthew was responsible for introducing the term "Father."[63] We should not think that Matthew was deliberately trying to misrepresent Jesus' teachings. He recognized how important the word "Father" had been for Jesus, and he probably knew that Jewish teachers were beginning to use the expression "Father in heaven." Matthew probably inserted the word "Father" into some of Jesus' sayings to emphasize how important this word had been for Jesus himself.

This kind of analysis does not mean that Matthew's evidence is always inaccurate when it is unsupported or contradicted by the other Gospels. But it does suggest that we must be cautious in using his evidence when we ask how often Jesus referred to God as "Father." The two earliest sources—Mark and the collection of sayings employed by Matthew and Luke—suggest that Jesus used the term "Father" relatively seldom.

To arrive at an understanding of Jesus' use of "Father," our best procedure will be to focus on a number of passages that occur in Mark or in the collection of sayings used by Matthew and Luke. We may supplement these occasionally by some passages that are probably authentic even though they occur only in Matthew or Luke. This procedure will limit the number of passages that we can take into consideration, but it will give us a reasonably accurate and comprehensive understanding of Jesus' usage.

It is clear, for instance, that Jesus spoke of God as "Father" in the sense of the ruler who wants his sons to obey his will, even to the extent of loving their enemies:

> But I say to you that hear, Love your enemies, do good to those who hate you, bless those who curse you, pray for those who abuse you. . . . Be merciful, even as your Father is merciful.
>
> (Luke 6:27–28, 36)

> But I say to you, Love your enemies and pray for those who persecute you. . . . You, therefore, must be perfect, as your heavenly Father is perfect.
>
> (Matt. 5:44, 48)

Jesus, of course, was not formulating a new view of God when he spoke of him as "Father" in the sense of ruler. We have met this general idea in the Old Testament and in Jewish writings, as well as in other religions and cultures of the ancient world. The distinctive element in Jesus' teaching here is the way he understands the significance of God's role as Father. He tells his followers, in effect, that they must be willing to practice love in all the relationships of their lives, even to the extent of loving their enemies and praying for them. Only if they are willing to do this can they think of God as their Father.

In a similar way Jesus spoke of God as "Father" when he dealt with the subject of forgiveness:

> And whenever you stand praying, forgive, if you have anything against any one; so that your Father also who is in heaven may forgive you your trespasses.
>
> (Mark 11:25)

> For if you forgive men their trespasses, your heavenly Father also will forgive you; but if you do not forgive men their trespasses, neither will your Father forgive your trespasses.
>
> (Matt. 6:14–15; cf. 18:35)

Jesus' teaching on forgiveness illustrates how closely the functions of ruler and helper are interrelated in the understanding of God as Father. God is the helper, who stands ready to forgive men their trespasses. But at the same time he is the ruler, who requires that men forgive one another before they can receive forgiveness from God himself. In a later chapter we will examine these aspects of forgiveness more closely. Here it is im-

portant to notice how the roles of ruler and helper coalesce in
Jesus' understanding of God as Father.

Jesus spoke of God as "Father" in the sense of helper when he
reassured his followers that God is aware of their needs:

> But if God so clothes the grass which is alive in the field today and tomor-
> row is thrown into the oven, how much more will he clothe you, O men of
> little faith? And do not seek what you are to eat and what you are to drink,
> nor be of anxious mind. For all the nations of the world seek these things;
> and your Father knows that you need them.
>
> (Luke 12:28–30; cf. Matt. 6:30–32)

Since this passage refers to God's control over the world of
nature, it represents an indirect reference to the idea that God
is creator of the world. A similar reference appears in Matt.
5:45, which states that God "makes his sun rise on the evil and
on the good, and sends rain on the just and the unjust." It is
very likely that Jesus regarded God as creator of the world, for
this idea would be part of his heritage from the Old Testament
and from Judaism. But in the present passage he refers to God's
rule over nature primarily to illustrate his main point, that God
cares for men and knows their needs. Jesus regarded God as the
creator of the world, but he did not especially emphasize this
idea in connection with his view of God as Father. In this respect his understanding of the term "Father" was very similar to
the view that we have noticed in the Old Testament and in
Judaism.

Jesus also spoke of God as "Father" in the sense of the helper
who stands ready to answer prayer:

> If you then, who are evil, know how to give good gifts to your children,
> how much more will your Father who is in heaven give good things to
> those who ask him?
>
> (Matt. 7:11; cf. Luke 11:13)

In this passage Jesus uses the "how much more" type of argument to reassure his hearers that they can trust in God to answer their prayers. Ordinary people, imperfect as they are, know
how to care for the needs of their children. How much more
then, Jesus asks, can men expect their heavenly Father to care
for them and respond to their prayers. Jewish teachers some-

times used this type of argument, which they called "from light to heavy"; i.e., if something is true in a lesser realm of experience, it will be all the more true in a greater realm. Jesus uses the argument here to illustrate the complete confidence that men can have in God as their heavenly Father.

We have seen that Jesus refers to God as "Father" to reassure his followers that God knows their needs and that God answers their prayers. Occasionally interpreters have regarded these two ideas as inconsistent. If God already knows our needs, is there any reason why we should pray about them? It does not seem necessary, however, to connect the two ideas in just this way. It would be more accurate to say that because God knows our needs, we can pray to him with complete confidence. God's knowledge of our needs, that is, actually becomes an encouragement to prayer.

We may look now at one other passage in which Jesus speaks of God as "Father" in the sense of helper:

Fear not, little flock, for it is your Father's good pleasure to give you the kingdom.

(Luke 12:32)

This passage is especially significant because it connects the terms "Father" and "kingdom." The Lord's Prayer itself makes a very similar connection. We have also seen that some Jewish prayers of Jesus' day addressed God as "Father" and "King." These prayers reflected the view that God is always king over his world. In a general sense Jesus shared this view. In his own teachings, however, he emphasized that God was now working in a special way to confirm his rule in the world. Thus in the present passage he assures his disciples that "it is your Father's good pleasure," or "your Father has resolved," to give the kingdom.

We have been looking at a number of passages in which Jesus used the expression "your Father" in speaking to his hearers. We have seen that he referred to God as "Father" in the sense of ruler or helper, but hardly at all in the sense of creator. We may look now at several further aspects of Jesus' use of the phrase "your Father."

It is significant that Jesus did not use the word "Father" very
often when he was speaking to other people about God. Although we cannot determine the exact number of instances,
there are relatively few in Mark and relatively few in the passages where Matthew is supported by Luke. Matthew himself, as
we have seen, has a tendency to insert "Father" when the parallel passages in other Gospels do not have it. Even if Matthew's
evidence may sometimes be accurate, it undoubtedly remains
true that Jesus used the term "Father" with considerable restraint. He regarded the word as so important that he used it
very carefully and selectively.

This observation is closely related to the question of whom
Jesus was addressing when he spoke to people of "your Father."
Unfortunately we cannot always determine who the audience
was in each particular case. Jesus' sayings were preserved orally
for some decades before they were written down, and the original occasion and audience were not always preserved along with
the sayings themselves. The Lord's Prayer itself illustrates how a
passage may appear in different settings in different Gospels.

Although we cannot always be certain of the audience, there
is some evidence that Jesus used the expression "your Father"
when he was speaking to his disciples rather than to people in
general. The Gospel accounts indicate that this was the case for
a number of the passages that we have examined (Mark 11:25;
Luke 11:13; 12:28–30; 12:32). We have also looked at a number of passages that come from Matthew's Sermon on the
Mount or Luke's Sermon on the Plain (Matt. 5:44, 48; 6:
14–15, 30–32; 7:11; Luke 6:27–28, 36). In these instances it
is uncertain whether Jesus was addressing his disciples or people
in general (cf. Matt. 5:1; Luke 6:17–20). Here too, however, it
is possible that Jesus originally addressed his sayings to his disciples.

The similarity between these sayings and the Lord's Prayer
helps to support this view. When Jesus used the expression
"your Father," he was reassuring his audience that God would
forgive them, God knew their needs, God would answer their
prayers, and God had promised to give them the kingdom.

These themes are closely related to the content of the Lord's Prayer or the spirit of heartfelt trust in which the Lord's Prayer is to be prayed. Since Jesus specifically intended the Lord's Prayer for his disciples, it is very likely that the sayings in which he spoke of "your Father" were also directed to the disciples.

Who then were these "disciples" to whom Jesus was speaking? Matthew speaks of Jesus' "twelve disciples" (10:1). Luke, however, says that Jesus chose the twelve "from" his disciples, and he also speaks of "a great crowd" of Jesus' disciples (6:13, 17). Matthew tends to limit the disciples to the twelve who were especially close to Jesus, while Luke uses the term in a broader sense to include all those who followed him. Undoubtedly the twelve were especially important as the group who accompanied Jesus during his ministry. In a broader sense it is also true, as Luke suggests, that Jesus' disciples included all the people who responded seriously to his proclamation of the good news of the kingdom of God.

It is also significant that when Jesus spoke of God as Father, he did not refer to any events in the past, such as the Exodus from Egypt, when God brought deliverance to his people. Nor did he speak directly of God as the Father of the Jewish people. He spoke instead of the things that God was doing now—seeking men who would be "merciful," caring for their needs, answering their prayers, and offering them the kingdom. Rather than define God's role as Father with reference to the past, Jesus called attention to the new ways in which God was working in the present and the new conditions of life that he was making possible.

In this way Jesus developed and extended the understanding of God as Father that we found in the Old Testament and Judaism. The Old Testament spoke of God as Father with particular reference to his acts of deliverance in the past on behalf of his people Israel. It also showed some tendency to restrict God's fatherhood to the "righteous" within Israel, and occasionally it expressed the belief that God, as Father, would act in the future to deliver or assist his people. Jewish writers tended to put more emphasis on the last two of these ideas.

Jesus no longer referred to the past in this connection, possibly because he felt that God's new actions completely overshadowed those of the past. Like the Jewish writers, he tended to restrict or individualize God's fatherhood, but he spoke of it in relation to those who responded to the kingdom rather than the "righteous" among the Jewish people. Like the Jewish writers also, he spoke of God's new ways of working, but he regarded these as beginning in the present rather than as simply expected for the future.

Jesus individualized the idea of God as Father in a way that made it implicitly or potentially universal. He referred to God as "your Father" when he spoke to those who responded to his proclamation of the kingdom and became his disciples. Most of these people were probably Jews, since the synoptic Gospels indicate that Jesus had very few contacts with non-Jewish people. But in principle anyone, Jewish or non-Jewish, could respond to the good news that Jesus brought. In this way Jesus removed the idea of God's fatherhood from its immediate relation to Judaism and redefined it so that it would apply to anyone who responded to his proclamation of God's kingdom.

At the same time, Jesus redefined the corporate conception of God's fatherhood that had been predominant in Old Testament times. The Old Testament writers had thought of God primarily as the Father of his people Israel. Jesus individualized the idea by relating it to anyone who responded to his message and became one of his followers. But he also made it a corporate conception, in a new sense, because he was establishing a new community of those who became his followers and experienced the new possibilities of life that God was bringing. He was calling together a new people of God who lived in grateful and obedient response to the rule of their heavenly Father.

We have been looking at various aspects of the expression "your Father," as Jesus used it in speaking to his disciples. Earlier in this chapter we examined the term *abba*, "Father," that Jesus used in his own prayers to God. We saw that this term expressed Jesus' close relationship to God, his commitment to God's will, and his trust in God's care and guidance. We may ask now about the relationship between Jesus' use of the word "Father" in private prayer and in speaking to his followers.

We may notice in this connection that Jesus never spoke of God as "our Father" in a comprehensive sense that would include both himself and his followers. He addressed God as Father, in the sense of "my Father," and he referred to God as "your Father" in speaking to his disciples, but he did not combine the two ideas into "our Father." His own relationship to God was unique, as his use of the term *abba* suggests. In and through Jesus, as he proclaimed God's rule in the world, his disciples could enter into a new and fuller relationship to God. Because he was the Son, in a unique sense, his disciples could receive a new form of sonship to God.[64] As the apostle Paul wrote a few years later, the followers of Jesus received "adoption as sons," so that they could address God as "Abba! Father!" (Gal. 4:5–6).

When Jesus instructed his followers to begin the Lord's Prayer with the address *abba*, he was inviting them to use a term that Jewish people would not have thought of using with regard to God. It was the everyday Aramaic word for father, drawn from the life of the home, intimate and at the same time respectful. Jesus used it, first of all, as a reflection of his close relationship with God and his sense of God's reality and presence. Then he gave his disciples the privilege of addressing God in this way because they were brought into a new and closer relationship with God as they responded to his proclamation of God's rule in the world.

The early followers of Jesus undoubtedly regarded it as a great privilege to address God with the everyday word *abba*. They used the word with a sense of awe, wonder, and gratitude. In this respect it was unfortunate that the Lord's Prayer was translated into other languages, which could not preserve the distinctive meaning of *abba*. It is very interesting to notice, however, that the liturgy of the Roman Catholic church still reflects some of this mood of wonder and gratitude in praying the Lord's Prayer. It introduces the prayer with the words, "We make bold to say [*audemus dicere*], 'Our Father.' "

Occasionally people today raise the question whether the
Lord's Prayer is a universal prayer that could be used by non-
Christians as well as Christians. Could a follower of Hinduism,
for example, pray this prayer? Or could the Lord's Prayer be-
come a common prayer for people of all faiths, enabling them
to worship together and express their common belief in God?
The fact that people of many different religions refer to God as
Father might suggest this possibility.

In a general sense it is possible that people of other religions
could pray the Lord's Prayer and find it meaningful in their
own lives. We have seen, however, that the word "Father" at
the beginning of the Lord's Prayer is not a commonplace of
religious thought. It represents the term *abba*, which expresses
the new relationship with God that men receive in and through
Jesus' proclamation of God's rule in the world. In this sense the
Lord's Prayer is a prayer for the followers of Jesus, and it has an
essential reference to Jesus himself. The prayer is universal in
the sense that the circle of Jesus' followers is potentially universal in scope. But the prayer itself, as Matthew, Luke, and the
Didache recognized, is specifically a prayer for Jesus' disciples.

We may look at one more aspect of the term "Father" before
we turn to a consideration of the "thou" petitions in the Lord's
Prayer. We have regarded the word as the address at the beginning of the prayer, and this of course is true. But the word *abba*,
"Father," also continues to govern the remainder of the prayer.
By expressing the new relationship that the disciples have with
God, it establishes the context within which they continue to
pray and trust that their prayer will be answered. Because the
disciples regard God as their Father, they can pray for the coming of his kingdom, the forgiveness of sins, or protection from
temptation. In this sense the word "Father" not only introduces
the prayer but makes the entire prayer possible.

Chapter Three

The "Thou" Petitions

Hallowed be thy name,
Thy kingdom come,
Thy will be done,
  on earth as it is in heaven.
       (Matt. 6:9–10)

Hallowed be thy name,
Thy kingdom come.

       (Luke 11:2)

Several stylistic features indicate that the "thou" petitions form a distinct section of the Lord's Prayer. In the Greek text they all follow the same word order, consisting of verb, noun, and possessive pronoun. They all have the verb in the third person singular, and they all have the pronoun "thy," referring to God. The petitions all follow one another directly, without any conjunctions such as "and" or "but." These stylistic characteristics suggest that the "thou" petitions are closely related to one another. They are addressed directly to God, and, as we will see, they probably refer to some aspect of God's own nature or activity.

Matthew has three petitions in this group, while Luke has two. In the first chapter of this study we looked at some of the reasons for thinking that Luke's version of the Lord's Prayer is probably closer to the original prayer that Jesus gave. We also saw that Jesus probably expected his followers to make some additions to the prayer as they used it and taught it to others. When Jesus said, "Pray then like this," he was evidently giving the Lord's Prayer as a model rather than an invariable formula. If Luke's form of the prayer is closer to the original, then the longer form in Matthew would reflect Jesus' own expectations that his disciples would make some additions or expansions to the prayer.

If Jesus gave the Lord's Prayer with only two "thou" petitions, it is possible that the early Christians expanded this part of the prayer by borrowing certain phrases and ideas from current Jewish prayers. The Kaddish, for example, begins in this way:

> Magnified and sanctified be his great name in the world,
>   which he created according to his will;
> and may he establish his kingdom in your lifetime and in
>   your days, and in the lifetime of all the house of Israel,
>   quickly and soon.[1]

This part of the Kaddish very probably goes back to Jesus' own time. It mentions God's name and kingdom, in the same order as in the first two "thou" petitions of the Lord's Prayer. It is very possible that Jesus knew the Kaddish and was influenced by it in formulating these petitions. The Kaddish also refers to God's will, although it gives this idea less prominence than the ideas of his name and kingdom. The early Christians, who came from a Jewish background and were undoubtedly familiar with the Kaddish, may have expanded the Lord's Prayer by adding the petition concerning God's will on the basis of the Kaddish.

Another prayer that may have influenced the early Christians in a similar way is the one attributed to R. Eliezer (about A.D. 100):

> Do thy will in heaven above
> and give peace of spirit to those who fear thee below [i.e., on earth],
> and do what is good in thine eyes.
> Blessed be thou, O Lord, who hearest prayer.[2]

This prayer refers to the doing of God's will in heaven and (implicitly) on earth. In this respect it is very similar to the third "thou" petition together with the explanatory phrase that follows: "Thy will be done, on earth as it is in heaven." This petition was undoubtedly added to the Lord's Prayer before A.D. 100, and we cannot be certain that R. Eliezer's prayer was earlier than this date. If the prayer is somewhat earlier than A.D. 100, or if it draws on earlier phrases and ideas, then the wording of the prayer may have had some influence on the formulation of the third "thou" petition in the Lord's Prayer.

In this chapter we will look at all three "thou" petitions, apart from the question whether Jesus originally gave two or three petitions in this section. Matthew's version of the Lord's

Prayer came into general usage at a very early time, and it has remained the predominant form throughout the history of Christianity. It is still substantially the same as the form that most Christians use today. By examining all three "thou" petitions, we can best understand the meaning of the prayer as we are familiar with it today.

Several questions of interpretation arise in relation to the "thou" petitions as a group. We may look at these briefly at this point before examining the individual petitions in detail. At the end of the chapter we will return to these questions and consider how they affect our understanding of the Lord's Prayer.

A first question, and probably the most important one, concerns the agent who is to carry out the actions indicated by the verbs. Do the "thou" petitions refer to God's actions, our actions, or both? Do they ask God to do something, do they express our commitment to do something, or both? When we pray "Hallowed be thy name," for example, are we asking God to hallow his name, are we indicating our own intention to hallow his name, or are both ideas involved? Because the "thou" petitions do not mention the agent, we need to ask by whom or through whom these actions are to take place.

A second question concerns the kind of future expectation that these petitions reflect. Do they refer to an "everyday" future or an eschatological future? In the first instance they would refer to the kind of future that comes as one day succeeds another in the ordinary course of events. They would refer to the future that comes simply with the passing of time, day after day, in the life of an individual person or a people. In the second instance the petitions would look forward to a special future, a new time of salvation, that God brings by intervening in history. This eschatological future is qualitatively different from the "everyday" type of future. It is not an outgrowth of the present, in the ordinary course of time, but it is a new time and a new situation that is brought into the present.

A third question concerns the scope of the "thou" petitions. Do they refer to the community of disciples alone, or do they also refer to the world in general? Is God's kingdom, for example, to be a reality only for the followers of Jesus, or is it something that will affect the lives of all people? In the next major division of the prayer, the "we" petitions, it is clear that the disciples are praying that God will meet their own needs as they live in the world. The problem is to determine whether the "thou" petitions have a broader scope that extends in some way to the world in general.

A fourth question concerns the relationship of the individual "thou" petitions to one another. Do they express different aspects of essentially the same idea, or do they express quite different ideas? When we pray that God's name may be hallowed, for example, is this essentially the same as asking that his kingdom may come and his will be done? If the "thou" petitions all express essentially the same idea, then it is less important whether the prayer has two or three petitions in this group. If they express different ideas, on the other hand, then the three petitions in Matthew would mean something more than the two petitions in Luke.

These are the main questions that we may keep in mind as we examine the individual "thou" petitions. Interpreters of the Lord's Prayer have differed widely with regard to the first two questions in particular. Some argue that the "thou" petitions refer to both God's actions and our own actions. In general, these interpreters also understand the petitions as referring to an "everyday" type of future.[3] Others believe that the "thou" petitions refer only to God's actions, and they understand the future in an eschatological sense.[4] With some exceptions, recent scholarship has shown a tendency toward this latter combination of ideas.

Hallowed be thy name

Occasionally these words have been regarded as an expression of praise or respect for God rather than a real petition. In this sense they would go more closely with the address, "Father," than with the petitions which follow the address. They would complete the address by indicating that the worshiper is approaching God reverently and preparing himself for prayer.

The RSV translation of Luke's form of the prayer actually suggests this interpretation by including these words in the same sentence as the address: "Father, hallowed be thy name."

It is very likely that we should regard these words as a genuine petition rather than an expression of praise or respect. As we noticed earlier, the words "Hallowed be thy name" have the same word order and stylistic characteristics as the other "thou" petitions. In particular we should notice that the word "hallowed" is not an adjective, as it might appear to be in English. It is part of the passive verb form, "hallowed be." It is parallel to the other verbs in this part of the prayer in the sense that all three have the same person, number, and mood. In this respect the comment of J. A. Bengel, the eighteenth century textual critic, is still significant: "The mood in 'hallowed be' has the same force as in 'come' and 'be done'; therefore petition, not praise, is expressed."[5]

What then does it mean to pray that God's name may be hallowed? We may notice first that in Old Testament thought a name is not simply an identification label to differentiate one person from another. It is an expression of innermost being, essential nature, and personal identity. It indicates who a person is, not simply how he is called. The name Jacob, for example, was understood to mean "supplanter." His brother Esau referred to this meaning of the name when he said, "Is he not rightly named Jacob? For he has supplanted me these two times. He took away my birthright; and behold, now he has taken away my blessing" (Gen. 27:36). Jacob acted as his name indicated, because his name expressed his essential character and personality.

In a similar way the "name" of God expresses his essential nature, especially as he reveals himself to men and acts on their behalf. Frequently the name of God is used as a synonym for God himself. To love God's name is to love God himself (Ps. 5:11), to bless his name is to bless him (Ps. 103:1), to praise his name is to praise him (2 Sam. 22:50). To know God's name is to know God as he makes himself known to men and offers them salvation:

> Because he cleaves to me in love, I will deliver him;
>   I will protect him, because he knows my name.
> When he calls to me, I will answer him;
>   I will be with him in trouble,
>   I will rescue him and honor him.
> With long life I will satisfy him,
>   and show him my salvation.
>
>   (Ps. 91:14–16)

When God acts "for his name's sake," he is acting in accordance with his essential nature. He chose Israel to be his covenant people that he might work through her to make known his salvation to all the earth (Gen. 12:3; Jer. 4:2; Isa. 49:6). To accomplish his redemptive purpose he will protect and preserve Israel, even when she is undeserving. He will act in accordance with his own nature and intentions:

> It is not for your sake, O house of Israel, that I am about to act, but for the sake of my holy name, which you have profaned among the nations to which you came . . . and the nations will know that I am the Lord, says the Lord God, when through you I vindicate my holiness before their eyes.
>   (Ezek. 36:22–23; cf. 1 Sam. 12:22)

In the Old Testament, God is both Lord of Israel and Lord of all the world. In a similar way his name is "great in Israel" (Ps. 76:1) and also "majestic . . . in all the earth" (Ps. 8:1). There is an inner connection between these two aspects of God's name. His name is known in Israel because he entered into a special relationship with Israel as his covenant people. His name is known throughout the world because he works through Israel to make himself known to all people:

> And my holy name I will make known in the midst of my people Israel; and I will not let my holy name be profaned any more; and the nations shall know that I am the Lord, the Holy One in Israel.
>   (Ezek. 39:7; cf. Ps. 96:1–6; Isa. 24:14–16; 59:19)

This close relationship between God and his name continued in Judaism after the Old Testament period. To bless God's name was to bless God himself (1 Enoch 61:11), and to trust in God's name was to trust in God himself as the source of forgiveness and salvation (Zadokite Fragments 9:54). Throughout much of the Old Testament period the Israelites had referred to God by his special name, Yahweh. In later times, out of a sense of reverence, the Jews avoided the use of this word. They developed a number of substitute expressions, of which one was simply "the Name." This specialized use of the word probably had no direct connection with the Lord's Prayer, but it does illustrate how closely God was identified with his name in Jewish thought.

The Old Testament and Jewish background suggests that in the Lord's Prayer the name of God signifies God himself. It is a way of referring to God in his innermost nature, especially as he reveals himself to men and acts on their behalf. It is not likely that the word refers to any particular name by which God is known, such as Yahweh or even *abba*. As we have seen, *abba* was the special word for Father that Jesus instructed his followers to use at the beginning of the Lord's Prayer. It expresses the new relationship with God that the disciples receive as followers of Jesus, and it enables them to pray the Lord's Prayer with confidence and hope. In this sense the word *abba* governs all the petitions in the prayer. But in the first petition the word "name" refers directly to God himself rather than any particular name by which he is known.

We may turn now to the verb "hallowed be" in the first petition. We should notice first that "hallowed" has the same meaning as "made holy" or "sanctified." These words can all be used in English to translate the same word in the Hebrew of the Old Testament or the Greek of the New Testament. The first petition, therefore, is a request that God's name may be hallowed, made holy, or sanctified.

Although the origin of the term is uncertain, the basic meaning of "holiness" in the Old Testament seems to be "separateness." Holiness is especially characteristic of God, because he is unique in himself, separate or different from everything else. The word points to the primal divine reality, mysterious and numinous, which can never be completely comprehended by the categories of human thought or experience. The prophet Isaiah expressed this awesome mystery of God's holiness in the words, "Holy, holy, holy is the Lord of hosts; the whole earth is full of his glory" (Isa. 6:3).

God's holiness does not mean simply that he is transcendent
or remote from the world of human affairs. He is the Holy One
in the midst of his people, who comes to bring them salvation
(Hos. 11:9). His way is holy, and he manifests his might among
the peoples of the earth (Ps. 77:13–14). His name is Holy, and
he dwells with those of a humble spirit:

> For thus says the high and lofty One
>   who inhabits eternity, whose name is Holy:
> "I dwell in the high and holy place,
>   and also with him who is of a contrite and humble spirit,
> to revive the spirit of the humble,
>   and to revive the heart of the contrite. . . ."
>
> (Isa. 57:15)

Some Old Testament writers also stress that God's holiness
expresses itself in his concern for justice and righteousness. In
this sense holiness is preeminently a moral quality. It means, on
the one hand, that God himself acts with righteousness: "But
the Lord of hosts is exalted in justice, and the Holy God shows
himself holy in righteousness" (Isa. 5:16; cf. Amos 4:2; Ezek.
20:9). On the other hand, God's holiness means that he expects
his people to be holy or righteous. Their holiness may take the
form of ritualistic practice, such as keeping the sabbath and
offering proper sacrifices. It may also express itself as righteousness and integrity in their social relationships. They are to re-
vere their parents, provide for the poor, treat one another
fairly, and love one another. These ritualistic and social aspects
of holiness are closely related in Old Testament thought. Both
are present, for example, in the nineteenth chapter of Leviticus
(cf. Exod. 19:5–6).

A number of writers, especially in the later parts of the Old
Testament, speak of God's name as holy.[6] The verb "sanctify,"
however, seems to occur only twice in connection with God's
name:

And I will sanctify my great name, which has been profaned among the
nations.

(Ezek. 36:23)

They will sanctify my name; they will sanctify the Holy One of Jacob.

(Isa. 29:23)

The passage from Ezekiel states that God himself will sanctify his name by acting on behalf of his people, so that the nations of the world will know that he is the Lord. The passage from Isaiah, on the other hand, indicates that the people will sanctify God's name by showing him reverence and obedience. The two passages illustrate the problem that we encounter in interpreting the first petition of the Lord's Prayer. In terms of the passage from Ezekiel, "Hallowed be thy name" would be a petition that God himself may sanctify his name by intervening in history. In terms of the passage from Isaiah, the phrase would mean that the disciples are to sanctify God's name by their way of life.[7]

A number of Old Testament passages also state that God will sanctify himself.[8] The meaning here is not that God will become holy, but that he will act in such a way as to demonstrate or manifest his holiness. He will restore his people to their homeland, and thus demonstrate that he is their holy God:

> When I gather the house of Israel from the peoples among whom they are scattered, and manifest my holiness in them in the sight of the nations, then they shall dwell in their own land which I gave to my servant Jacob.
> (Ezek. 28:25)

The thought that God sanctifies himself is equivalent to the idea that he sanctifies his name, since God's name represents God himself. The two expressions occur together in Ezek. 36:23: "And I will sanctify my great name . . . when through you I sanctify myself before their eyes." We should note that in the Old Testament, God is always the subject of the verb "sanctify" when it appears in this form.[9] God sanctifies himself by manifesting his intrinsic holiness, but people or things do not sanctify themselves. This Old Testament usage may well be parallel to the first petition of the Lord's Prayer. It suggests that God himself is the agent in the phrase "Hallowed be thy name." In this case the phrase would be a petition that God may sanctify himself, or manifest his holiness, by intervening in history and bringing a new time of salvation to men.

Later Jewish writers believed that God's name could be sanctified either by God himself or by men. For this reason they do

not give us any direct help in interpreting the first petition of
the Lord's Prayer. Sometimes, indeed, they combined both
thoughts in a single passage:

Sanctify thy name, for the sake of those who sanctify thy name.[10]

(God says to Israel,) If you sanctify my name, so I will also sanctify my
name for your sakes.[11]

How then are we to understand the petition, "Hallowed be
thy name"? There is, of course, some Old Testament and Jewish
background for understanding it to mean that men should sanctify God's name by their obedience to his commandments. In
itself this idea can be very meaningful for the followers of Jesus
as a way of understanding the significance of their own actions.
At this point, however, we must ask specifically what Jesus
meant in the first petition of the Lord's Prayer. Several considerations indicate that he regarded it as a petition that God
himself might act by manifesting his holiness.

A first consideration in this connection is that this meaning is
more appropriate for a real petition. A petition is a request
directed to God, asking him to do something. In this sense it is
more natural to understand the first petition of the Lord's
Prayer as a request that God may act by sanctifying his name in
the world.

A second consideration concerns the use of the passive verb
form, "be hallowed" or "be sanctified." Jewish writers sometimes used the passive voice as an indirect and respectful way of
referring to God. Jesus himself used the passive in this way
about forty times.[12] In the Sermon on the Mount, for example,
he said, "Blessed are those who mourn, for they shall be com-
forted" (Matt. 5:4). He meant that God would comfort those
who mourn, but he employed the passive voice as an indirect
way of referring to God's action. Jesus very probably used the
passive in this same way in the petition, "Hallowed be thy
name." The petition therefore would mean "sanctify thy name"
or "manifest the holiness of thy name."

This use of the passive, thirdly, is parallel to the passive of the
verb "sanctify" in the Old Testament. As we noted above, God

is always the subject when the verb is used in this form. God is sanctified, or sanctifies himself, by acting in some way that reveals or vindicates his holiness.

A fourth consideration is that this understanding of the first petition is consistent with the meaning of the second petition, "Thy kingdom come." We will examine the meaning of the second petition very shortly. At this point we may note, however, that God's kingdom can be established only by God himself. Men can respond to it and seek to make it the center of their lives, but they themselves do not bring it. The kingdom comes as it is given and established by God. Since the three "thou" petitions are so closely related in form and structure, it is likely that God is the agent throughout. God sanctifies his name, just as he brings his kingdom.

Thy kingdom come

The central theme of Jesus' ministry was his proclamation that the kingdom of God was at hand. Through his teachings and his actions he called attention to the kingdom and illustrated various aspects of its meaning. For this reason it might seem rather surprising that the petition for the coming of the kingdom does not appear at the very beginning of the "thou" petitions in the Lord's Prayer. We might expect it to be the first petition because the idea of the kingdom of God was so central in Jesus' ministry.

The explanation appears to lie in the meaning of the word "kingdom." In Greek, Hebrew, and Aramaic the "kingdom" of God means primarily the kingship, sovereignty, reign, or ruling activity of God. We usually use the word "kingdom" in English translation, but it would be more accurate to use one of these other terms, such as "reign," to depict God's role or activity as king.

The name of God, as we saw earlier, refers to God's own innermost nature. The kingdom or reign of God refers to his activity as king. Since his innermost nature finds expression in his activity, it is appropriate for the petition concerning God's name to precede the petition concerning his kingdom. The petitions do not refer to two distinct events, but their sequence reflects the logical basis of God's activity. Together, they ask God to express his innermost nature and thus assume his role as king.

The idea of the kingdom of God has its roots in the Old Testament, although the phrase as such does not occur there. The Old Testament writers describe God as king, they proclaim that he reigns, and sometimes they use the expressions "his kingdom" or "thy kingdom" with reference to God. In these ways they refer to God's reign or activity as king, which is the primary meaning of the phrase "kingdom of God."

The Old Testament writers speak of God as king in connection with his activities of leading the Israelite people out of slavery in Egypt, revealing himself at Mount Sinai, and giving the law through Moses (Num. 23:20–24; Deut. 33:2–5).[13] For the first two centuries after their settlement in Canaan, the Israelites generally felt that they could not have a human king because the Lord was their king. When some of the people asked Gideon to become king, he reflected the prevailing attitude by replying, "I will not rule over you, and my son will not rule over you; the Lord will rule over you" (Judg. 8:23). When the Israelites finally decided to choose a human king, about 1020 B.C., there was still considerable opposition on the grounds that this step would represent a rejection of the Lord as king (1 Sam. 8:7; cf. Hos. 8:4).

The Israelites continued to regard God as king, however, even after they had established the human kingship. They stressed that God's kingdom was everlasting: "Thy kingdom is an everlasting kingdom, and thy dominion endures throughout all generations" (Ps. 145:13; cf. Exod. 15:18). They also believed that his kingship extended, at least in principle, over the created world and all the peoples of the earth: "The Lord reigns; let the peoples tremble! . . . The Lord is great in Zion; he is exalted over all the peoples" (Ps. 99:1–2; cf. 1 Chron. 29:11; Pss. 22:27–28; 93:1–4; 95:3–5; 96:10–13; 97:1–9; 103:19). The Israelites believed that their divine king had the attributes of glory and power, but they also emphasized his ethical qualities of mercy and love, righteousness and truth (Ps. 145:8-11; 1 Chron. 29:11; Pss. 96:3-4, 10-13; 97:6-12; 98:9; 99:4).

In these ways the Israelites expanded their understanding of God as king. He was not simply the God of a particular group of people, the God who guided them in their wanderings and protected them in times of danger, but he was the righteous king over all the earth. It is uncertain how early the Israelites enlarged their conception of God's kingship in this way. Many of the Psalms that reflect these ideas are classified as Enthronement Psalms, because they celebrate the Lord's "enthronement" as king over the world. These Psalms had their setting in the worship services of the Jerusalem temple, and they may well have come into use at an early period.

Although the Israelites regarded God as king over the entire world, they also realized that many nations did not acknowledge him as king. Sometimes, indeed, the Israelites themselves were oppressed by foreign powers, and they were not free to worship God as the sole ruler over their lives. For these reasons they looked forward to a time when God would effectively establish his rule over their own country and over all the peoples of the world. According to this eschatological view of the kingdom, God would intervene in human history to bring a new time of salvation and assert his rule over the world (Obad. 21; Dan. 2:44; 7:18, 22, 27).

After the close of the Old Testament period, the Jews held several different views of the kingdom of God. They continued to believe that God, in principle at least, was king over the whole world because he had created the world (Enoch 9:4-5; 84:2-3). They also believed that God was ruler over individual persons who took upon themselves "the yoke of the kingdom of God." People acknowledged God's kingship in this way by confessing him as the one true God and giving obedience to his law. These two themes were expressed in the confession of faith known as the Shema, which consisted of passages from the books of Deuteronomy (6:4-9; 11:13-21) and Numbers (15:37-41). For this reason the expression "take upon oneself the kingdom of God" became a way of referring to the recitation of the Shema.[14] This understanding of the kingship of God emphasized his present rule in the hearts of men.

In addition to these views of God's universal rule over his creation and his individual rule in the hearts of faithful men, Jewish writers also developed the eschatological conception of God's kingdom. They looked forward to the time when God would manifest his rule over the entire earth, so that all peoples would acknowledge him as the one true God. When the Jews were in subjection to a foreign power, such as Rome, they frequently believed that the coming of God's kingdom would bring release from bondage and the restoration of the Jewish state.

This political aspect of the eschatological hope appears in a number of Jewish sources, although not in all. In the Psalms of Solomon and in the Eighteen Benedictions it is combined with the hope for a Davidic messiah, who will restore the Davidic throne in Israel:

> But we hope in God, our deliverer;
> For the might of our God is for ever with mercy,
>   And the kingdom of our God is for ever over the nations
>   in judgment. . . .
> Behold, O Lord, and raise up unto them their king, the son of David,
>   At the time in which Thou seest, O God, that he may reign over
>   Israel Thy servant.
>
> (Ps. Sol. 17:3–4, 23) [15]

> Have mercy, O Lord our God, on Jerusalem thy city, and on Zion the habitation of thy glory, and on the kingdom of the house of David, the Anointed One of thy righteousness.
>
> (Eighteen Benedictions, no. 14)

Some Jewish writings make no reference to a Davidic messiah but represent God as acting directly to establish his kingdom. Although this type of expectation is not political, it is still nationalistic in the sense that it focuses on the vindication of the Jewish people. The Assumption of Moses is especially interesting in this respect, for it was written in Palestine during the lifetime of Jesus:

And then His kingdom shall appear throughout all His creation,
And then Satan shall be no more,
And sorrow shall depart with him . . .
For the Most High will arise, the Eternal God alone,
And He will appear to punish the Gentiles,
And He will destroy all their idols.
Then thou, O Israel, shalt be happy . . .
And God will exalt thee.

(Asmp. M. 10:1, 7–9) [16]

Since the idea of the kingdom of God was already present in Judaism, it is clear that Jesus did not invent the term. He did not, however, simply take it over and use it with the same range of meanings that it had in Judaism. He used the phrase almost exclusively in its eschatological sense to designate the new time of salvation that God was bringing. At the same time he redefined the scope of the kingdom, the requirements for admission into the kingdom, and the time of its coming. To see how this was so, we may look at a number of passages from the first three Gospels that illustrate Jesus' understanding of the kingdom of God.

Jesus made the idea of the kingdom of God the central and governing theme of his ministry. He spoke of it in sayings and parables, and he illustrated its meaning through his actions. According to Mark, he began his ministry with the proclamation, "The time is fulfilled, and the kingdom of God is at hand; repent, and believe in the gospel" (Mark 1:15; cf. Matt. 4:17). This proclamation of the kingdom continued to govern his entire ministry. In this way Jesus gave the idea a central significance that it did not have in Judaism.

Jesus regarded the kingdom as God's gift to men. God alone could establish the kingdom, and he had graciously decided to do so: "Fear not, little flock, for it is your Father's good pleasure to give you the kingdom" (Luke 12:32). The kingdom was God's to give, and he granted it according to human needs (cf. the parable of the laborers in the vineyard, Matt. 20:1–16). As God's gift, the kingdom was more than anyone could earn, even the most righteous (cf. the parable of the servant's wages, Luke 17:7–10). Jesus' view of the kingdom as God's gift differed from the Jewish idea of "taking upon oneself the kingdom of

God," which emphasized the obedience that men owe to God as king.

Because the kingdom was a gift, Jesus believed that God was making it available to all who genuinely recognized their need for it. God was offering the kingdom to the ordinary people of the day, who could not follow all the detailed regulations of religious practice that Jewish law required (cf. Matt. 5:3; Luke 6:20). He was also offering it to religious and social outcasts, such as tax collectors and sinners (cf. Mark 2:15–17). Indeed, Jesus warned that God would take the kingdom away from religious leaders such as the Pharisees and give it to those who recognized their need and responded to it (cf. the parable of the great supper, Luke 14:15–24). To express this idea Jesus frequently used the imagery of a meal as a symbol for the kingdom of God. Jewish sources also used this symbolism, but they never represented sinners or other outcasts as participants in the meal.

Although God's kingdom was a gift, Jesus emphasized that men must make a proper response. They must receive the kingdom like a child, with openhearted trust and gratitude (cf. Mark 10:15). They must give themselves to the kingdom with single-minded devotion and loyalty (cf. Luke 9:62). They must regard the kingdom as more important than all other concerns in life, like the merchant who sold all that he had, to buy one pearl of great value (cf. Matt. 13:44–46). They can lose their opportunity to enter the kingdom if they do not do God's will (cf. Matt. 7:21–23; Luke 6:46; 13:26–27). Jesus did not think that men could earn or build the kingdom, for it always remained God's gift. But he did think that men could exclude themselves from the kingdom if they did not respond appropriately and seek to live according to God's will.

A number of Jesus' sayings and actions indicate that he regarded the kingdom of God as already partially present in his ministry. The reality of the kingdom was already making itself felt, for example, in the healings that he performed: "But if it is by the Spirit of God that I cast out demons, then the kingdom of God has come upon you" (Matt. 12:28; cf. Luke 11:20). In a similar way Jesus referred to his healings when he replied to the question sent by John the Baptist (cf. Matt. 11:2–6; Luke 7:18–23). When his disciples reported that they had performed similar healings, Jesus said to them, "I saw Satan fallen like lightning from heaven" (Luke 10:18). Since God's rule signified health and wholeness of life for men, Jesus' healings were signs that the kingdom was already making itself effective in the world.

Other aspects of Jesus' ministry also indicate that he regarded the kingdom as partially present. He ate a meal with tax collectors and sinners, using the symbolism of table-fellowship as a sign of the kingdom (cf. Mark 2:15–17; Matt. 11:19; Luke 7:34). He released his disciples from the obligation of fasting because they were living in a new and joyful time, just as wedding guests were freed from fasting regulations when they celebrated a wedding (cf. Mark 2:18–19). He told the Pharisees that the kingdom of God was not coming with signs to be observed, "for behold, the kingdom of God is in the midst of you" (Luke 17:21). He was probably referring to the kingdom of God when he told his disciples that they were seeing and hearing things that many people of past generations could not see or hear (cf. Matt. 13:16–17; Luke 10:23–24). In a similar way he was probably referring to the kingdom when he said that "something greater" than the temple, the prophet Jonah, or King Solomon was now present (cf. Matt. 12:6, 41–42; Luke 11:31–32).

Some of Jesus' sayings and actions, on the other hand, indicate that he regarded the kingdom of God as still to come in its fullness. He told his disciples that "there are some standing here who will not taste death before they see the kingdom of God come with power" (Mark 9:1). He believed that there would be a resurrection to a new life (cf. Mark 12:18–27), and he warned the unrepentant Jewish cities that there would be a time of judgment (cf. Matt. 11:20–24; Luke 10:13–15). At the Last Supper he used the symbolism of a meal to depict the kingdom as it would be in the future: "I shall not drink again of the fruit of the vine until that day when I drink it new in the kingdom of God" (Mark 14:25). He also used the symbolism of

table-fellowship to indicate that Gentiles would have the opportunity to share in the kingdom: "Men will come from east and
west, and from north and south, and sit at table in the kingdom
of God" (Luke 13:29; cf. Matt. 8:11).

Some of Jesus' parables seem to combine the present and the
future aspects of the kingdom. This is the case, for instance,
with the parables of the sower, the mustard seed, and the leaven
(cf. Mark 4:1–9, 30–32; Matt. 13:33; Luke 13:20–21). Although these parables have been interpreted in a number of
different ways, they probably emphasize the contrast between
the present beginnings of the kingdom and its wondrous nature
and extent in the future. Jesus used these parables to combine
both aspects of the kingdom and reassure his followers that God
would indeed continue to establish his reign in the world.

The evidence from the first three Gospels indicates that Jesus
regarded the kingdom of God as already partially present in his
own ministry, but still to come in its entirety in the future.
This view is sometimes known as *inaugurated eschatology*. It is
"eschatological" because it understands the kingdom as a new
time of salvation that God is bringing. It is "inaugurated" because it regards God's reign as already beginning.[17] In this respect Jesus' understanding of the kingdom differed notably
from that of Judaism. When Jewish writers referred to the
kingdom in an eschatological sense, they regarded it as solely
future.

Jesus' view of the kingdom of God as already inaugurated
provides the context in which we should understand the second
petition of the Lord's Prayer, "Thy kingdom come." We are
praying that God will establish his reign completely over the
earth, just as he began to establish it in the life and ministry of
Jesus. The petition refers to the future aspect of the kingdom,
but this aspect in turn is grounded in the fact that the kingdom
is already partially present. In this respect the petition for the
coming of God's kingdom is not simply a general idea that anyone could have expressed. It has an intrinsic connection with
the ministry of Jesus, through whom God began to establish his
kingdom.

The first two "thou" petitions have essentially the same scope and meaning. God's "name" signifies his innermost nature, and God's "kingdom" signifies the expression of his nature in his effective rule over the world. But both are genuine petitions that ask God to do something. Both are eschatological, in the sense that they ask God to bring his new time of salvation. Both have reference to the community of disciples, to whom God offers his salvation. At the same time both have a worldwide scope, since God hallows his name before all the world, and his reign extends over all the world. The petitions refer to both the disciples and the world at large because Jesus never imposed nationalistic limitations on discipleship. People from every nation of the earth can become his followers by recognizing their need for the salvation that he proclaimed, responding in faith to the heavenly Father that he made known, and committing themselves to live in accordance with his teachings.

Thy will be done, on earth as it is in heaven

It is very likely that this third petition, which occurs only in Matthew, has essentially the same meaning as the other two "thou" petitions. If this is so, then the third petition is a prayer that God may accomplish his will throughout the earth, just as he sanctifies his name and brings his kingdom. The third petition, like the first two, is a prayer that God may bring his new time of salvation. The words "on earth as it is in heaven" indicate explicitly that God's salvation is to extend throughout all of his creation.

The word translated "will" in the Lord's Prayer corresponds to terms in the Old Testament that mean God's "delight" or "purpose," his "favor" or "will." It was God's delight or purpose, for example, to deliver his people from oppression in Egypt and give them a new homeland (Ps. 135:5–12). In a similar way, at the time of the Babylonian exile, it was his purpose to deliver his people:

> My counsel shall stand,
> and I will accomplish all my purpose. . . .

> I bring near my deliverance, it is not far off,
> and my salvation will not tarry.
> (Isa. 46:10, 13; cf. 44:28; 48:14)

God's "favor" or "will" can also mean his gracious intention to have mercy on his people and give them his help:

> In a time of favor I have answered you,
> in a day of salvation I have helped you.
> (Isa. 49:8; cf. 60:10; 61:2)

These examples from the Old Testament illustrate how God himself accomplishes his will by bringing salvation to his people. In addition to this idea, however, we also find the view that people do God's will by obeying his law or following the guidance of his spirit:

> I delight to do thy will, O my God;
> thy law is within my heart.
> (Ps. 40:8)

> Teach me to do thy will,
> for thou art my God!
> Let thy good spirit lead me
> on a level path!
> (Ps. 143:10)

These two ways of understanding God's will continue in Judaism. Sometimes it is God himself who accomplishes his will or purpose. The Kaddish, for example, says that God created the world "according to his will." The prayer of R. Eliezer, quoted at the beginning of this chapter, begins with the petition, "Do thy will in heaven above." In a Jewish writing of the second century B.C. we find the thought, "As it may be (God's) will in heaven, so he will do" (1 Macc. 3:60). In all of these instances God himself executes his will by bringing something to pass.

On the other hand, the idea that men are to do God's will is also widespread in Judaism. The expression "to do God's will" was commonly used in the Palestinian synagogues.[18] R. Judah b. Tema, who probably lived around the middle of the second century A.D., said, "Be bold as a leopard, swift as an eagle, fast as a stag, and strong as a lion, to do the will of thy Father

which is in heaven" (Aboth 5:23). A saying of R. Simon b. Eliezer, about A.D. 200, speaks of doing God's will in connection
with the effect on his "name":

When the Israelites do the will of God, then his name is made great in the
world . . . and when they do not do his will, then his name is, as it were,
profaned in the world.[19]

These examples illustrate the problem that we encounter in
interpreting the third petition of the Lord's Prayer. When we
pray, "Thy will be done," do we mean that it should be done by
God himself or by us? In the first instance we are asking God to
carry out his purposes. In the second instance we are expressing
our own intention to carry out God's will in our lives. Both
interpretations, as we have seen, can be supported by Old
Testament and Jewish usage.

Apart from the Lord's Prayer, Jesus apparently did not refer
very often to God's will or speak of "doing" God's will. In his
prayer in Gethsemane he said, "Thy will be done" (Matt.
26:42; cf. Luke 22:42). Jesus was praying here that God would
carry out his plans for the salvation of men. In a similar way he
remarked, at an earlier point in his ministry, "So it is not the
will of my Father who is in heaven that one of these little ones
should perish" (Matt. 18:14). In both of these instances God
himself is the agent who carries out his will by bringing salvation to men.

Jesus also indicated that it was important for men to do God's
will: "Whoever does the will of my Father in heaven is my
brother, and sister, and mother" (Matt. 12:50; cf. Mark 3:35;
Matt. 7:21; 21:31). There is no reason to question that Jesus
spoke of doing God's will in this way. We should notice, however, that most of these examples come from Matthew, who was
especially concerned about the moral responsibility of Christian
life. Mark expresses this idea only once (3:35), and Luke not at
all. It is possible that Matthew gave special prominence to the
idea of doing God's will, even though it does have a basis in
Jesus' own teaching.[20]

If Matthew added the third "thou" petition, or found it in

the tradition that was available to him, it is possible that he understood it as a commitment on the part of men to carry out God's will in their lives. In this case the petition would mean, "May we do thy will." We cannot be certain, of course, that Matthew understood it this way, but this understanding would be consistent with Matthew's emphasis throughout his Gospel on the idea of doing God's will.

If Jesus himself included the third "thou" petition, on the other hand, it is more likely that he understood it as a prayer that God would accomplish his will by bringing salvation to men. The third petition then would have essentially the same meaning as the first two, which it so closely resembles in form and structure. As in the first petition, the passive voice of the verb would be an indirect, respectful way of referring to God's action. The petition, therefore, could be paraphrased, "Do thy will."

Before we leave the third petition, we may notice that the exact meaning of the second part is uncertain. This is usually translated into English, "on earth as it is in heaven." This translation suggests that God already reigns in heaven and executes his will without opposition. In this sense the third petition would be a prayer that God may accomplish his purposes on earth, as they are already perfectly executed in heaven.

The Greek words for this part of the petition read literally, "as in heaven, also upon earth." These words can be understood in the way just indicated, and probably most interpreters give them this meaning. They can also be understood, however, to mean "both in heaven and upon earth." This translation would imply that God's will is still opposed by supernatural beings or forces in heaven, as well as upon earth. The third petition then would be a prayer that God may accomplish his purposes in both heaven and earth.[21]

Some New Testament writers reflect the view that heaven is the abode of evil forces or powers, as well as good, and that salvation will ultimately involve the recreation of heaven as well as earth.[22] A rather late Jewish prayer suggests that the idea of opposition to God in heaven was also known to Judaism:

May it please thee, Eternal One, Our God, to make peace in the family
above and in the family below. . . .[23]

Jesus' own usage, according to the first three Gospels, suggests
that he thought of heaven as the domain in which God already
reigned without any kind of opposition. He almost always spoke
of heaven simply as the abode of God, with little or no indication that forces existed there which were opposed to God's
will.[24] Jesus spoke, for example, of receiving a great reward in
heaven (Matt. 5:12) and storing up treasures in heaven (Matt.
6:20). He looked up to heaven when he prayed (Matt. 14:19),
and he said that the message of John the Baptist was "from
heaven" rather than "from men" (Matt. 21:25). He warned
against swearing "by heaven," because it was the throne of God
(Matt. 23:22). Sometimes he even used the word "heaven" as
an indirect way of referring to God, as when he told the parable
of the prodigal son who said, "I have sinned against heaven"
(Luke 15:18).

These examples of Jesus' usage indicate that the translation
"on earth as it is in heaven" represents a correct interpretation
of this part of the third petition. The petition assumes that
God's will is already perfectly accomplished in heaven, and it
prays that this situation may be extended from heaven to earth.
The entire petition could be paraphrased, "Do thy will on
earth, as it is already done in heaven."

At the beginning of this chapter we looked at four questions
of interpretation that arise in relation to the "thou" petitions as
a group. We may return to these briefly at this point and ask
what significance they have for our understanding of the Lord's
Prayer.

The first question concerned the agent who is to carry out the
actions indicated by the verbs. In all probability, as we have
seen, the "thou" petitions are directed to God as the agent. God
himself is being asked to sanctify his name, bring his kingdom,
and perform his will. The passive voice in the first and third
petitions is an indirect way of referring to divine action.

It is natural to ask, of course, whether Jesus did not want
people to sanctify God's name, respond to his sovereignty, and

do his will. In a general sense there can be no doubt that he wanted them to live their lives in this way. But our problem is to determine what Jesus meant when he gave the Lord's Prayer to his disciples. The second petition is especially decisive at this point, for Jesus never said that the kingdom can be brought or built by men. Only God can bring the kingdom, and in a similar way it is very probable that God is also being asked to sanctify his name and do his will.

If this interpretation is correct, it suggests that Jesus regarded God's actions as prior to men's in the structure of religious experience. Men can try to live faithfully within their present situation, but only God can bring a new situation with new possibilities of life. In the Lord's Prayer, Jesus was instructing his followers to pray that God would bring in his new time of salvation with all of its possibilities for fullness of life under his rule.

The question of agency is closely related to the second question, which concerns the type of future expectation reflected by the "thou" petitions. Since these petitions ask God to do something, it is very likely that they refer to the new time of salvation that he is bringing to men. They refer, that is, to an eschatological rather than an "everyday" type of future. Here again the second petition is especially determinative. Jesus almost always spoke of the kingdom of God in an eschatological sense, as a new time and a new state of affairs that "comes" into the world.

The "thou" petitions ask God to complete the work of salvation that he has already begun through the ministry of Jesus. Thus they refer to an eschatological future, but a future that is partially present. For this reason they still relate to daily life. Christians live their lives, day by day, in memory and hope. They recall the significance of Jesus' ministry, relate it to their own experience, and look forward to the completion of God's salvation. When they pray that God will sanctify his name, bring his kingdom, and do his will, they are asking him to complete the work that he has already begun and in which they already share.

With regard to the third question, concerning the scope of
the "thou" petitions, we have seen that they refer to the community of disciples and also to the world at large. The petitions
ask God to continue the work of salvation that he has already
inaugurated. In this sense the petitions have reference most directly to the followers of Jesus, for they already share in God's
salvation and are looking forward to its completion. At the same
time the scope of the petitions extends in principle to the entire
world. God sanctifies his name before the world, and he is king
over the whole world. Because Jesus never imposed nationalistic
limitations on discipleship, people from all the nations of the
world can become his disciples and share in the kingdom that
he proclaimed.

If this interpretation is correct, it means that there is an intercessory aspect to the "thou" petitions. In part, of course,
those who offer these petitions are praying that they themselves
may share more fully in God's salvation. But at the same time
they are praying on behalf of all people throughout the world.
They are asking God to assert his sovereignty over the entire
world, so that all men may have the opportunity to acknowledge him as Lord and King.

The fourth question that we raised at the beginning of this
chapter concerns the relationship of the individual "thou" petitions to one another. We have seen that they all refer to God's
work of bringing in his new time of salvation. In this sense they
all express essentially the same idea, and it is relatively unim-
portant whether Jesus gave the Lord's Prayer with two or three
petitions in this group. The shorter form in Luke, that is, has
essentially the same meaning as the longer form in Matthew.

The petitions differ in the sense that they depict different
aspects of the idea that God is bringing his salvation. God's
"name" signifies his essential nature and personal identity. The
petition that God may sanctify his name stands first, because
God's work of salvation originates within his innermost being.
God's "kingdom" is the expression of his nature in his effective
reign over the world, and his "will" is the work that he per-

forms in his role as king. These two petitions refer more specifically to God's external relationship to his world.

The "thou" petitions reflect a logical progression of thought
as they refer first to God's own nature and then to his relationship to the world and his activity in the world. Yet they all have
reference to God's work of salvation. Collectively, they reveal
the internal self-consistency of God's work by showing the intrinsic connection between his nature and his activity. They
indicate that God reveals himself in his activity, and his activity
in turn is the expression of his innermost nature.

The scope of the "thou" petitions extends beyond the community of disciples to include the world at large. The "we"
petitions, on the other hand, reflect the situation of Jesus' followers as they pray that their own needs may be met. In the
next chapter we will turn to these "we" petitions and examine
the requests that Jesus' followers make as they already share in
the kingdom of God and look forward to its completion.

Chapter Four

The "We" Petitions

Give us this day our daily bread,	Give us each day our daily bread,
And forgive us our debts,	And forgive us our sins,
as we also have forgiven our debtors,	for we ourselves forgive everyone who is indebted to us,
And lead us not into temptation,	And lead us not into temptation.
But deliver us from evil.	
(Matt. 6:11–13)	(Luke 11:3–4)

The major sections of the Lord's Prayer are arranged according to a logical progression of thought that relates the sections to one another and gives unity to the prayer as a whole. In the address, the disciples of Jesus call upon God as *abba*, "Father," a term that reflects the new relationship of sonship to God that they have received through Jesus. This new relationship with God continues to govern the entire prayer. In the "thou" petitions the disciples ask God to complete the work of salvation that he has initiated through the ministry of Jesus. Then in the "we" petitions they ask God to satisfy their own needs as they live within the new time of salvation and look forward to its completion. The sections of the prayer are distinct from one another, yet each prepares the way for the next. Together, they give the Lord's prayer an internal spiritual unity that seems to have no parallel elsewhere.

A number of stylistic characteristics indicate that the "we" petitions form a distinct division of the Lord's Prayer. They all have the words "us" or "our," referring to the followers of Jesus who are offering the prayer. They all have the verb in the second person singular. They all begin with some word other than the verb, and they are joined together by the conjunctions "and" or "but." The "thou" petitions, as we have seen, differ from the "we" petitions in all these respects.

In the first chapter of this study we looked at a number of

83

reasons for thinking that the shorter form of the prayer in Luke may be more authentic than the longer form in Matthew. In general these considerations still apply to the "we" petitions. In some instances, however, the specific words that Matthew uses probably reflect more accurately the Aramaic terms that Jesus used when he gave the prayer. This is especially the case in the "we" petitions, and we will notice a number of examples when we examine the individual petitions in detail.

Give us this day our daily bread

Matthew's version of this petition reads literally, "give us this day our daily bread." Luke's version, on the other hand, has "keep giving us day by day our daily bread." In Greek it is possible to make a distinction between the simple "give" and the progressive form "keep giving." In Aramaic, however, this distinction is not possible. Matthew's version represents one way of interpreting the underlying Aramaic, while Luke's version represents another. The adverbial expressions are consistent with the forms of the Greek verbs. Matthew has "give . . . this day," and Luke has "keep giving . . . day by day."[1]

Matthew's version seems to envision a situation in which Christians live one day at a time and ask God each day to provide for their needs. It may also reflect the belief that the kingdom of God will come very soon in all of its fullness. In contrast, Luke's version seems to reflect the view that Christians should continually ask God for help on a daily basis as they live within an ongoing period of time. Luke does believe that the kingdom will come, but he apparently does not think that it will necessarily come in the near future. He is concerned about the meaning of Christian life as it continues for an indefinite time before the complete coming of the kingdom.

Although we cannot be certain, it is likely that Matthew's wording expresses more accurately the meaning of the fourth petition as Jesus gave it. Jesus instructed his followers to live one day at a time, placing their trust in God's protective care (cf. Matt. 6:25–34). According to Mark, he also taught that the kingdom of God would come "with power" within the lifetime

of the present generation (Mark 9:1).[2] Even if Jesus did not set
a specific time limit to the coming of the kingdom, it is likely
that the wording "give . . . this day" represents his outlook more
accurately than "keep giving . . . day by day." In a more general
sense, both translations reflect Jesus' teachings about trust in
God's goodness and confidence that he will answer prayer and
provide for men's needs.

At first sight the meaning of the phrase "daily bread" would
seem to be self-explanatory. It would signify the bread and
other food that we need for physical nourishment. By extension
it could also include other necessities of life, such as clothing
and shelter. It might even include other factors that make life
worthwhile, such as good friends, meaningful work, or a health-
ful environment. Whether or not we generalize the phrase to
include all the conditions and circumstances that contribute to
well-being, the basic meaning of the phrase would seem to be
clear.

It is very possible that the phrase "daily bread," understood
literally or more generally, represents at least a part of Jesus'
meaning in the fourth petition. But we need to examine the
phrase carefully and try to determine its meaning. It is quite
possible that the phrase should not be translated as "daily"
bread.

The Greek word *epiousios*, which is usually translated
"daily," poses a special difficulty. The word occurs in the text of
the Lord's Prayer, as we have it in Matthew, Luke, and the
Didache. But it does not occur elsewhere in the New Testament. Two possible examples of *epiousios* have been found in
Greek writings outside the New Testament, but both of these
are uncertain.[3] Under these circumstances, therefore, we cannot
analyze the meaning of the word in the Lord's Prayer by com-
paring it with examples in other writings.

Another approach is to examine the derivation of *epiousios*
itself. It is a compound word in Greek, made up from the
preposition *epi*, "for," and some other word. In general, according to the derivation that we assume, there are four major possibilities for the meaning of *epiousios*. It could mean (1)

"necessary for existence," (2) "for today," (3) "for the coming day," or (4) "for the future."[4] This approach makes us aware of the possible meanings of the word, which we can keep in mind as we look at a number of references to bread or food in the Bible. But unfortunately this approach itself is inconclusive, since we cannot be certain which derivation is correct.[5]

Since other examples of *epiousios* do not seem to exist, and the derivation of the word is uncertain, it will be more helpful to examine references to bread or meals in the Old Testament, Judaism, and Jesus' ministry. We will be especially concerned, of course, to look at Jesus' own understanding of food and meals. Then perhaps we will be in a better position to know which possible meaning of *epiousios* is most appropriate to modify the word "bread" in the Lord's Prayer.

The writers of the Old Testament refer to food in several ways that are important as background for our study of the fourth petition in the Lord's Prayer. Sometimes, for example, they speak of food as a gift that God provides for men in his providential care for his creation:

> Happy is he whose help is the God of Jacob,
>   whose hope is in the Lord his God,
> who made heaven and earth,
>   the sea, and all that is in them;
> who keeps faith for ever;
>   who executes justice for the oppressed;
>   who gives food to the hungry.
> (Ps. 146:5–7)

> Let them thank the Lord for his steadfast love,
>   for his wonderful works to the sons of men!
> For he satisfies him who is thirsty,
>   and the hungry he fills with good things.
> (Ps. 107:8–9)

> Remove far from me falsehood and lying;
>   give me neither poverty nor riches;
>   feed me with the food that is needful for me.
> (Prov. 30:8)

These examples suggest that God provides food for men as part of his love and concern for the world that he created. This

attitude toward food is rather general, in the sense that it has no
reference to specific incidents in the history of the Israelite people. It assumes that food is necessary for human life and that
God provides for men according to their needs. This understanding of food would suggest that *epiousios* in the Lord's
Prayer has the meaning "necessary for existence." In this case,
Jesus would be instructing his disciples to pray that God would
provide them with the bread or food that is necessary to sustain
human life.

The account of the manna in the wilderness reflects the more
specific idea that God provides food for his people day by day.
When the Israelites complained about the lack of food in the
wilderness, Moses reassured them that God would give them
food:

Then the Lord said to Moses, "Behold, I will rain bread from heaven for
you; and the people shall go out and gather a day's portion every day, that
I may prove them, whether they will walk in my law or not." . . . and in
the morning dew lay round about the camp. And when the dew had gone
up, there was on the face of the wilderness a fine, flake-like thing, fine as
hoarfrost on the ground. . . . Morning by morning they gathered it, each
as much as he could eat; but when the sun grew hot, it melted. On the
sixth day they gathered twice as much bread, two omers apiece; and when
all the leaders of the congregation came and told Moses, he said to them,
"This is what the Lord has commanded: 'Tomorrow is a day of solemn
rest, a holy sabbath to the Lord; bake what you will bake and boil what
you will boil, and all that is left over lay by to be kept till the morning.' "
(Exod. 16:4, 13–14, 21–23)

Each morning God provides a supply of manna that lasts only
for that day. On the sixth morning he gives a supply that lasts
for two days, since the following day is the sabbath day of rest. If
Jesus had this account in mind when he gave the Lord's Prayer,
it would suggest that *epiousios* means "for today" or possibly
"for the coming day." Jesus would be instructing his disciples,
that is, to ask each day for their daily supply of food, just as the
Israelites in the wilderness received their daily food from God.

Several passages in the Old Testament use the symbolism of
food or meals to depict a coming time of salvation. When the
Israelites were in exile in Babylon, for example, one of the
prophets proclaimed that God would soon set the exiles free

and restore them to their homeland. He used the symbolism of a meal to describe this wonderful event of deliverance and restoration in which the exiles would share:

> Ho, every one who thirsts,
>   come to the waters;
> and he who has no money,
>   come, buy and eat!
> Come, buy wine and milk
>   without money and without price.
> Why do you spend your money for that which is not bread,
>   and your labor for that which does not satisfy?
> Hearken diligently to me, and eat what is good,
>   and delight yourselves in fatness.
>
> (Isa. 55:1–2; cf. 65:13–14)

This passage, written about 540 B.C., refers especially to the good fortune that the Israelite exiles will receive. Since it is addressed to "every one who thirsts," it may also refer to non-Israelites who come to know and worship Israel's God. Another passage, which is probably several centuries later, speaks of a meal that is clearly intended for all the peoples of the world:

> On this mountain the Lord of hosts will make for all peoples a feast of fat things, a feast of wine on the lees, of fat things full of marrow, of wine on the lees well refined. And he will destroy on this mountain the covering that is cast over all peoples, the veil that is spread over all nations. He will swallow up death for ever, and the Lord God will wipe away tears from all faces, and the reproach of his people he will take away from all the earth; for the Lord has spoken.
>
> (Isa. 25:6–8)

This passage uses the symbolism of a meal to depict a wonderful time in the future when God will completely assert his sovereignty over the world. The passage focuses on Israel, for "this mountain" is probably Mount Zion in Jerusalem (cf. Ps. 48:1–3). In this sense the passage is nationalistic in its outlook. But at the same time it anticipates that all the peoples of the world will share in God's salvation. The feast is intended for all peoples, and the "veil" of ignorance, which prevents them from knowing God, will be removed. The passage is strongly eschatological, since it states that death itself will be abolished. God's will, which is for life rather than death, will prevail without opposition. The passage also reflects the sense of joyfulness that people will feel when they share in this wonderful time of salvation.

Many of the features of this passage, as we shall see, recur in Jesus' own use of meal imagery. If Jesus was thinking of food in this way when he gave the Lord's Prayer, then *epiousios* would have the meaning "for the future." When the disciples pray, "give us this day our bread for the future," they would be asking God to grant them, here and now, some of the gifts of the wonderful time of salvation that is still to come in its fullness.

As in the Old Testament, Jewish writings sometimes express the view that food is a gift which God provides in his providential care for the world. In the Eighteen Benedictions, for example, this idea takes the form of asking God to bless the agricultural produce of the current year: "Bless this year unto us, O Lord our God, and fill the world with the treasures of thy goodness. Blessed art thou, O Lord, who blessest the years" (Eighteen Benedictions, no. 9). The first benediction of grace at mealtime refers at greater length to God's role as king of the universe and creator of the world:

Blessed art thou, O Lord our God, king of the universe, who feedest the whole world with thy goodness, with grace, with loving kindness and tender mercy: thou givest food to all flesh, for thy loving kindness endureth for ever. Through thy great goodness food hath never failed us: O may it not fail us for ever and ever for thy great name's sake, since thou nourishest and sustainest all beings and doest good unto all, and providest food for all thy creatures whom thou hast created. Blessed art thou, O Lord, who givest food unto all.[6]

In addition to this general acknowledgement that God provides food in his love for his creation, Jewish writers sometimes use the imagery of food or meals as a symbol for a coming time of salvation. In this way they continue and develop the type of symbolism that appears in the late Old Testament passage, Isa. 25:6–8. The Jewish sources vary widely with regard to the type of food that is to be eaten, the kind of future that is anticipated, the presence or absence of a messiah, and the attitude toward non-Jewish peoples. We may examine several examples, however, and look for themes that they have in common.

One of the Jewish sources gives a vivid picture of the miraculous fruitfulness of the earth in the time to come:

The earth also shall yield its fruit ten thousandfold and on each (?) vine there shall be a thousand branches, and each branch shall produce a thousand clusters, and each cluster produce a thousand grapes, and each grape produce a cor of wine. And those who have hungered shall rejoice. . . . And it shall come to pass at that self-same time that the treasury of manna shall again descend from on high, and they will eat of it in those years, because these are they who have come to the consummation of time.[7]

Two features of this passage are especially important. One is the idea that those who share in this meal will "rejoice." This reaction is not the happiness that comes from some good fortune in everyday life, but the sense of joyfulness that comes from sharing in the time of salvation. The other important feature is that God will once again give the people manna to eat. Just as he once gave them manna in the wilderness, at the time of Moses, now he will give them manna again in the new time of salvation. The idea of manna has been transposed into an eschatological setting to symbolize the time to come.

One of the Dead Sea Scrolls, produced by the sectarian Jewish community near the northwestern shore of the Dead Sea, speaks of a meal of bread and wine that the community will enjoy when God sends the Messiah. In accordance with the priestly nature of the Dead Sea community, the presiding priest will take precedence over the Messiah:

This is the session of the men of renown, summoned to the meeting for the council of the community, when God begets the Messiah. . . . And if they are met for the common table or to drink the wine, and the common table is set, and the wine is mixed for drinking, let not any put forth his hand on the first of the bread or the wine before the priest . . . and next the Messiah of Israel shall put forth his hand on the bread. And then all the congregation of the community shall pronounce the blessing, each according to his rank. And according to this statute they shall do for every meal when there are met as many as ten men.[8]

In addition to being priestly in its nature and organization, the Dead Sea community stressed the importance of ritual purity. It excluded from its fellowship "anyone afflicted in his flesh, injured in his feet or hands, lame or blind or deaf or dumb. . . ."[9] These unfortunate people could have no hope of sharing in the life of the community or participating in the meal that it would hold when the Messiah came. As we shall see, this attitude stands in sharp contrast to Jesus' own treatment of those who were socially and religiously disinherited by the society of the time.

Among Jewish rabbis the idea of a meal or banquet was a rather common symbol for the time of salvation or "the world to come":

This world is like a porch before the world to come. Make thyself ready in the porch, that thou mayst enter into the banqueting-hall.[10]

For your meal there is an end, but for the meal of our God, which he will prepare in the future for the righteous, there is no end.[11]

In the future God will prepare a meal for the righteous, on the day when he will manifest his grace to the seed of Isaac. After they have eaten and drunk, they give the cup of blessing to our father Abraham, that he may pronounce a eulogy.[12]

He who serves God up to the day of his death, will satisfy himself with bread, namely the bread of the world to come.[13]

As the first redeemer (i.e., Moses), so the last redeemer (i.e., the Messiah). . . . As the first redeemer brought down manna . . . so will also the last redeemer bring down manna.[14]

Several features of this symbolism are especially noteworthy. The first example stresses that men must make proper preparation in this world if they wish to share in the future salvation. The second indicates that this time of salvation will be everlasting. The third mentions the patriarch Abraham as a participant in the meal. Only the beginning is quoted here, but the passage goes on to mention Isaac, Jacob, Moses, Joshua, and David. The fourth passage above specifically speaks of "bread" as a symbol for the time of salvation. This is especially suggestive, of course, for our interpretation of the Lord's Prayer. The fifth example expresses the Jewish belief that the Messiah will bring manna when he comes.

We have been looking at a number of examples from the Pseudepigrapha, the Dead Sea Scrolls, and the rabbinic writings in which food or meals symbolize the coming time of salvation. The various examples of Jewish usage have two characteristics in common. They usually stress, first, that only the righteous can be admitted to the eschatological banquet. The righteous are Jews who faithfully observe all the detailed regulations of the Jewish laws and meet the requirements of ceremonial and ritual cleanliness. There is no Jewish example of the eschatological banquet symbolism that offers admission to the outcasts of the time, such as tax collectors and sinners, or to the "lame or blind or deaf or dumb."

The second characteristic is that the banquet symbolism in Judaism always has reference entirely to the future. The meal will take place in the future, and it symbolizes a time of salvation that is to come in the future. In the last chapter, when we examined Jesus' view of the kingdom of God, we saw that it could be described in terms of inaugurated eschatology. This is a way of saying that Jesus regarded the time of salvation as already beginning in the present, although it was still to come in its fullness in the future. There is, however, no Jewish example of the banquet symbolism that regards the future time of salvation as already partially present.

We may turn now to Jesus' understanding of food and ask how it may contribute to our interpretation of the meaning of *epiousios* in the Lord's Prayer. Since the meaning of this word is so uncertain, it is especially important that we try to relate it to Jesus' sayings or actions that have reference to food or meals. More generally, we also need to relate it to Jesus' ministry as a whole, which centered about the proclamation of the kingdom of God and its meaning for men.

As in the Old Testament and Judaism, Jesus occasionally referred to food as a sign of God's providential care for his creation. In the Sermon on the Mount, for instance, he taught, "But if God so clothes the grass of the field, which today is alive and tomorrow is thrown into the oven, will he not much more clothe you, O men of little faith? Therefore do not be anxious, saying, 'What shall we eat?' or 'What shall we drink?' or 'What shall we wear?' " (Matt. 6:30–31; cf. 5:44–45). Jesus trusted in God's care for the world, and he taught others to do the same. But he apparently did not emphasize this idea. We find, at least, very few examples in his teaching.

Much more frequently, Jesus referred to food or meals in relation to his proclamation of the new time of salvation that God was inaugurating. In this way he used banquet imagery as a symbol for the kingdom of God. When we examine the accounts of Jesus' ministry, it is surprising how often this symbolism appears in his sayings and parables and in the actions that he performed. It is also reflected in comments that other people made about him. The banquet imagery may be regarded as the primary symbol that Jesus used to illustrate his understanding of the kingdom of God.

Sometimes Jesus used this symbolism to depict conditions in the kingdom when it would arrive in its fullness in the future:

> I tell you, many will come from east and west and sit at table with Abraham, Isaac, and Jacob in the kingdom of heaven, while the sons of the kingdom will be thrown into the outer darkness; there men will weep and gnash their teeth.
>
> (Matt. 8:11–12; cf. Luke 13:28–29)

The people who will come "from east and west" are Gentiles who will be admitted to the kingdom. The idea that non-Jewish peoples will share in the future time of salvation is not entirely absent from Jewish sources. It occurs in two Jewish representations of the eschatological banquet (1 Enoch 62:14; cf. 50:2–3; Testament of Levi 18:8b–11). The distinctive element in Jesus' saying is that "the sons of the kingdom" will be rejected from the banquet. These are the righteous Jews, and perhaps especially the Jewish leaders, who would expect to have some prior claim to the kingdom. Jesus warns that they have failed in their responsibility to God and will therefore be refused admission to the banquet of the future.

In the Beatitudes, Jesus also used the symbolism of a meal to refer to the future aspect of the kingdom:

> Blessed are you poor,
> for yours is the kingdom of God.
> Blessed are you that hunger now,
> for you shall be satisfied.

> Blessed are you that weep now,
>   for you shall laugh.
> >   (Luke 6:20–21; cf. Matt. 5:3–4, 6)

Jesus did not mean that it was blessed to be hungry. In a land afflicted by poverty and overpopulation, he knew that this was not so. He was reassuring the poor and hungry that God's kingdom was coming and all their needs would be satisfied. In this sense he promised them that they would be happy. The connection between satisfying hunger and rejoicing is especially interesting because it occurs, as we have seen, in some Jewish representations of the eschatological banquet.

At the Last Supper, Jesus also used the symbolism of a meal to refer to the future aspect of the kingdom:

> Truly, I say to you, I shall not drink again of the fruit of the vine until that day when I drink it new in the kingdom of God.
> >   (Mark 14:25; cf. Matt. 26:29; Luke 22:15–16, 18)

At this point Jesus is thinking especially of himself and his disciples. He is looking beyond his impending death and expressing his own hopes for the future, when he will share in the complete kingdom of God. According to Matthew's version of this passage, Jesus promised the disciples that he would drink the fruit of the vine "with you" in the kingdom. The other accounts do not have these words. Whether or not Jesus actually used them, he undoubtedly included the disciples in his hopes for the future.

In the three passages that we have examined so far, Jesus used the symbolism of a meal to depict the future aspect of the kingdom of God. Jewish sources, as we have seen, always referred to the future when they used the banquet symbolism. In this sense Jesus' usage here is parallel to that of the Jewish writers. The distinctive element in Jesus' usage is the sense of authority that underlies his statements. He warns the Jewish leaders that they will be excluded from the eschatological banquet, he promises the poor and the hungry that they will be admitted, and he expresses his confidence in the future as it will affect himself and his disciples. Jesus does not explicitly claim to be the Messiah in these passages, but they rest on his messianic authority.

Jesus also used the symbolism of a meal to show that the time of salvation was already partially present in his own ministry, bringing new possibilities of life to men and challenging them to modify their customary ways of thinking. This use of the symbolism reflects Jesus' view that the kingdom of God was already beginning to be established in the world. It stands in sharp contrast to Jewish usage, which always employed the symbolism of the eschatological banquet to refer to the future.

One of the most important incidents in this respect is the occasion on which Jesus ate a meal with tax collectors and sinners:

And as he sat at table in his house, many tax collectors and sinners were sitting with Jesus and his disciples; for there were many who followed him. And the scribes of the Pharisees, when they saw that he was eating with sinners and tax collectors, said to his disciples, "Why does he eat with tax collectors and sinners?" And when Jesus heard it, he said to them, "Those who are well have no need of a physician, but those who are sick; I came not to call the righteous, but sinners."

(Mark 2:15–17; cf. Matt. 9:10–13; Luke 5:29–32)

The tax collectors were Jews who collected customs taxes from their fellow Jews on behalf of the Romans. In general, the Jews despised these tax collectors and regarded them as collaborators or traitors. They distrusted them so much that they did not allow them to give evidence in courts of law. The "sinners" in the Gospels were people whose lives were immoral (cf. Luke 7:37) or else simply the common people of the day who did not know and observe all the detailed regulations of the Jewish law (cf. John 7:49). Strict Jews like the Pharisees avoided contact with sinners in either sense of the term. Yet Jesus actually sought out tax collectors and sinners and shared a meal with them.

It is quite possible that Jesus ate meals with tax collectors and sinners on a number of occasions. He was the guest of Zacchaeus, a chief tax collector (Luke 19:1–10). At another meal he accepted the presence of "a woman of the city, who was a sinner" (Luke 7:37). He was accused of being "a glutton and a drunkard, a friend of tax collectors and sinners" (Matt. 11:19; cf. Luke 7:34). The scribes and the Pharisees were offended that

"this man receives sinners and eats with them" (Luke 15:2).
The various accounts in the Gospels suggest that Jesus made a
practice of eating meals with such people. They indicate further
that the "righteous" Jews of the day found this practice especially offensive.

When Jesus ate with tax collectors and sinners, he was using
the symbolism of the eschatological banquet to show that the
kingdom of God was already becoming a reality in the world.
Here and now the tax collectors and sinners had the opportunity to enter the kingdom and experience its meaning for their
lives. They could not claim to be virtuous, but they could recognize their need for God's forgiveness and grace. They were
rejected by the Jewish religion of the time, but now they received the opportunity for a renewed relationship with God (cf.
Matt. 21:31–32; Luke 18:9–14). When we realize the significance of Jesus' actions, we can understand why the Jewish leaders found them so offensive. Jesus was declaring that the
kingdom of God was already partially present, and he was making it available to the outcasts and the disinherited of the day.

In other ways too Jesus used the symbolism of the eschatological banquet to call attention to the present aspect of the kingdom of God. In the parable of the great supper, he referred to
the kingdom as a "great banquet" or a "marriage feast" (Luke
14:15–24; Matt. 22:1–10). The Jewish leaders would be rejected from the kingdom, but the social and religious outcasts of
the time have the opportunity to enter it. Luke's version of the
parable describes these people as "the poor and maimed and
blind and lame" (Luke 14:21). This is almost exactly the same
group, as we have seen, that the Dead Sea community wanted to
exclude from its eschatological banquet: "lame or blind or deaf
or dumb." Jesus included the people whom the Dead Sea community deliberately rejected as ritually unclean.

Jesus' attitude toward fasting also reflects his belief that food
or meals can symbolize the kingdom of God:

Now John's disciples and the Pharisees were fasting; and people came and
said to him, "Why do John's disciples and the disciples of the Pharisees

fast, but your disciples do not fast?" And Jesus said to them, "Can the
wedding guests fast while the bridegroom is with them?"

(Mark 2:18–19a; cf. Matt. 9:14–15a; Luke 5:33–34)

A wedding celebration was a joyful time in Judaism when the
usual regulations for fasting were suspended. In a similar way,
Jesus argues, the new time of salvation has come. It is a joyful
time, when fasting would be inappropriate, and thus he does
not require his disciples to fast. Their eating and drinking symbolizes their participation in the kingdom of God to the extent
that it is a present reality. This sense of joyfulness appears, as we
have seen, in some Jewish representations of the eschatological
banquet and in Jesus' teachings in the Sermon on the Mount. It
appears here in connection with Jesus' remark about fasting,
which refers to the present aspect of the time of salvation.

Jesus' use of the banquet symbolism with reference to the
present aspect of the kingdom of God reflects a unique messianic authority that had no parallel in Judaism. Through this
symbolism he declares that the time of salvation is already becoming a reality. He eats with tax collectors and sinners, giving
them the opportunity to share in God's kingdom and thereby
offending the Jewish leaders of the day. He invites "the poor
and maimed and blind and lame" to enter the kingdom. Because the time of salvation is a time of rejoicing, he releases his
disciples from the obligation of fasting. This use of the symbolism of the eschatological banquet is so distinctive that it cannot
be understood apart from the new and unprecedented messianic
authority of Jesus' own ministry.

We have seen that Jesus usually regarded food or meals as a
symbol of the kingdom of God. His use of this symbolism suggests that the puzzling word *epiousios* in the Lord's Prayer
would mean "for the future." The entire petition would be,
"Give us this day our bread for the future." In this sense the
followers of Jesus would be praying that they may receive,
here and now, some of the benefits of the future time of salvation. The phrase "this day" refers to the present aspect of the
kingdom, and "bread for the future" symbolizes the future

aspect of the kingdom. This interpretation of *epiousios* is consistent with Jesus' use of the eschatological banquet symbolism throughout his ministry. It is also consistent with his understanding of the kingdom of God as partially present and still to come in its fullness.

The translation "our bread for the future" has the same meaning as "our bread for the morrow," which the RSV gives in a footnote to the Lord's Prayer. In Judaism the word "tomorrow" could mean the future, or the coming time of salvation. This particular translation rests on some comments by the church father Jerome:

In the Gospel called according to the Hebrews for "supersubstantial" bread I found *mahar*, which means "of the morrow;" so that the sense is, Our bread of the morrow, that is, of the future, give us this day.

(Commentary on Matt. 6:11)

In the Hebrew Gospel according to Matthew it is thus: Our bread of the morrow give us this day; that is, the bread which thou wilt give us in thy kingdom, give us this day.

(Tractate on Ps. 135)[15]

This "Gospel according to the Hebrews," to which Jerome refers, was apparently a rather late Aramaic document based on the Gospel of Matthew. There is considerable disagreement among New Testament scholars whether this document actually gives independent evidence for the wording that Jesus used in the Lord's Prayer.[16] For this reason it is preferable to interpret the fourth petition of the Lord's Prayer in relation to Jesus' other references to food or meals throughout his ministry. Jerome's comments are important in the sense that they give some possible support to the view that the fourth petition speaks of "bread for the future" or "bread for the morrow."

When we pray the Lord's Prayer, we are accustomed to use the words "daily bread." If we understand the fourth petition to speak of "bread for the future," does the petition still have any reference to the bread that we eat day by day? The answer to this question lies in Jesus' understanding of the significance of food and meals. Food can be a symbol for the kingdom of God, as it is already partially present and as it is still to come in its fullness. The ordinary food that we eat can be a sign of this new time of salvation, with its sense of joyfulness, forgiveness, and fellowship with one another and with God. In this way the Lord's Prayer is still related to everyday life. It still refers to the bread that we eat day by day, but it places this bread within a broader context that has its basis in Jesus' proclamation of the kingdom of God.

And forgive us our debts, as we forgive our debtors

The versions of this petition in Matthew and Luke both differ somewhat from the wording that is usually used today. Matthew has literally, "And forgive us our debts, as we also have forgiven our debtors." Luke's version has, "And forgive us our sins, for we ourselves forgive everyone who is indebted to us." To understand the meaning of the petition as accurately as possible we must try to determine which version is more likely to be correct.

The term "debts" in Matthew reflects the Aramaic idiom by which "debts," in a monetary sense, could also be used to mean "sins." The Greek word for debts does not ordinarily have this additional meaning and can be understood as "sins" only by those who are aware of the Aramaic term that it represents. Matthew keeps the term "debts" because he is writing for Christians of a Jewish background who can understand that it means "sins" in this context. Luke has simply changed to the Greek word for sins to make the meaning clear for Christians of a Gentile background who might not understand the term "debts." In this instance, therefore, Matthew's version reflects the original wording of the prayer more closely than Luke's.

Sometimes people use the word "trespasses" rather than "debts" when they pray the Lord's Prayer today. "Trespasses" does not occur in any of the early versions of the prayer. Matthew, however, uses this term in the passage that he places after the Lord's Prayer (Matt. 6:14–15; cf. Mark 11:25). Since Matthew connected this passage so closely with the Lord's Prayer, he clearly regarded "trespasses" as having the same meaning as "debts." At some point "trespasses" evidently crept into the

Lord's Prayer itself on the basis of its occurrence in Matt. 6:14–15. Those who use the word today are not changing the meaning of the prayer, although "debts" would be preferable in the sense that it does occur in Matthew's text of the Lord's Prayer.

Matthew's version of the petition for forgiveness joins the two clauses by the expression "as also," while Luke has simply "for." Both expressions can represent ways of interpreting the underlying Aramaic term.[17] Matthew's wording is preferable, however, because it makes a much closer connection between the two clauses. The first clause speaks of divine forgiveness, and the second speaks of human forgiveness. Later we shall try to determine exactly how these forms of forgiveness are related to each other. But it is clear that they are closely connected, and in this sense Matthew's wording is to be preferred.

Matthew's version has a past tense, "we have forgiven," while Luke's has the present, "we forgive." Here again these readings can represent different ways of interpreting the Aramaic verb, which has no specific reference to time.[18] Matthew's form of the verb is more consistent with the other verbal forms in the Lord's Prayer. It also emphasizes that a person must actually forgive his debtors if God's forgiveness is to become real for him. The present tense in Luke is vaguer, and it could shade off into an indefinite promise for the future. Here again, therefore, Matthew's wording is preferable to Luke's.

In the Old Testament the most common term for forgiveness or pardon means literally to "send away." This term is used, for example, in the following passages:

> Seek the Lord while he may be found,
>   call upon him while he is near;
> let the wicked forsake his way,
>   and the unrighteous man his thoughts;
> let him return to the Lord, that he may have mercy on him,
>   and to our God, for he will abundantly pardon.
>
> (Isa. 55:6–7)

> For thou, O Lord, art good and forgiving,
>   abounding in steadfast love to all who call on thee.
>
> (Ps. 86:5)

. . . for we do not present our supplications before thee on the ground of our righteousness, but on the ground of thy great mercy. O Lord, hear; O Lord, forgive. . . .

(Dan. 9:18–19)

These passages make it clear that the writers of the Old Testament thought of God as one who does indeed forgive or "send away" the sins of his people. At the same time they illustrate various aspects of God's forgiving activity. Because God is holy and righteous, he looks for genuine repentance on the part of those who seek his forgiveness. In this sense God's forgiveness can become real for men only when they desire a renewed relationship with him and seek to live according to his will. But God's forgiveness is more than simply a reward for the repentance or the righteousness that men show. It has its basis in God's own nature, his "steadfast love" or his "great mercy" toward his people. In the final analysis, God's forgiveness is always a gift that exceeds anything that men can deserve or earn.

Jewish writers continued to emphasize that men must earnestly desire God's forgiveness. In particular, they stressed that men must be willing to forgive others if they wish to receive forgiveness from God:

Forgive the wrong of thy neighbor, and then your sins will be forgiven when you pray.

(Sirach 28:2)

R. Judah (ca. 150) said in the name of R. Gamaliel (ca. 90): "As often as you are merciful (in forgiving your neighbor), the All-Merciful has pity on you (in forgiving you)."[19]

At the same time, Jewish writers also stressed that forgiveness is a gift that has its source in God's own love or mercy. Petition for God's forgiveness was an important part of Jewish prayers in the first and second centuries:

Forgive us, our Father, for we have sinned against thee; blot out our transgressions from before thine eyes. Blessed art thou, O Lord, who forgivest much.

(Eighteen Benedictions, no. 6)

Our Father, our King, according to thy great mercy remit our promissory notes [literally, all the accounts of our sins].[20]

With some modifications, Jesus' own view of forgiveness included both of these ideas. He stressed that a man must be willing to forgive others, and he also emphasized that God's forgiveness is a gift that cannot be earned. He expressed the first idea, for example, in his answer to a question raised by Peter:

Then Peter came up and said to him, "Lord, how often shall my brother sin against me, and I forgive him? As many as seven times?" Jesus said to him, "I do not say to you seven times, but seventy times seven."

(Matt. 18:21–22; cf. Luke 17:4)

Some Jewish rabbis taught that a man should forgive another person three times; others said that he should forgive seven times. Jesus also teaches the obligation to forgive other people, but he argues that acts of forgiveness cannot be counted up until a particular limit is reached. Genuine forgiveness cannot be defined or restricted in this way. Forgiveness seeks to restore the wholeness of relationships between persons, rather than simply satisfying the requirements of a particular regulation.

In a similar way Jesus taught that in the final analysis God's forgiveness is always a gift. God gives it to men according to their needs, and they can never really claim that they have earned it:

A certain creditor had two debtors; one owed five hundred denarii, and the other fifty. When they could not pay, he forgave them both.

(Luke 7:41–42)

So you also, when you have done all that is commanded you, say, "We are unworthy servants; we have only done what was our duty."

(Luke 17:10)

Some Jewish teachers believed that good deeds helped to counterbalance the effect of bad deeds in God's sight.[21] In this sense they thought that human achievements could influence God's forgiveness, even though his forgiveness in the final analysis was a gift that would not be completely earned. Jesus, of course, also stressed the importance of doing God's will. As the Sermon on the Mount illustrates, his teachings in this respect could be even more stringent than those of contemporary Jewish teachers. But Jesus did not teach that men could balance their good deeds against their bad deeds as a way of influencing God's forgiveness. He believed that men cannot really claim to deserve such forgiveness, no matter how many good deeds they have performed. They remain "unworthy servants" who realize that God's forgiveness is a gift far surpassing anything that they could earn by their own achievements.

Jesus accepted the current Jewish ideas that a person must be willing to forgive others, and that God's forgiveness is a gift which rests ultimately on his love and mercy. He differed from some Jewish teachers in rejecting any kind of calculation that would seek to set limits on human forgiveness or influence God's forgiveness by balancing good deeds against bad deeds. In each case he evidently felt that this kind of calculation would obscure the true meaning of forgiveness as the restoration of meaningful relationships among men or between men and God.

Jesus' understanding of forgiveness was also distinctive in a further respect. As part of his proclamation of the kingdom of God, he declared that God's forgiveness of sins was already becoming a reality. He told the paralytic at Capernaum, "Your sins are forgiven" (Mark 2:5; Matt. 9:2; Luke 5:20). He said the same thing to the "woman of the city, who was a sinner," when he was eating in the home of a Pharisee (Luke 7:48). In each case the bystanders were astonished that Jesus should speak in this way. As they understood it, this unexpected kind of forgiveness could come only in the future as part of the new time of salvation. Jesus declared that this forgiveness of sins was already a reality, here and now. Just as he healed the sick and ate with tax collectors and sinners, he proclaimed God's forgiveness as a sign of the present aspect of the kingdom of God.

In this way Jesus understood forgiveness of sins within the framework of inaugurated eschatology. The new time of salvation would be a time of forgiveness, when men would live in the presence of God with the certain knowledge that he had forgiven them and taken them back to himself. But this new time of salvation was already beginning, and forgiveness of sins

was already becoming a reality for men. Thus Jesus could tell
sinners, here and now, that their sins were forgiven.

This understanding of forgiveness is especially important for
our interpretation of the Lord's Prayer. When we ask God to
forgive us our debts, or sins, we are asking him to complete the
work of forgiveness that he began through Jesus' own ministry.
We know that we are still imperfect, and we know that we do
not yet live completely in God's kingdom. For these reasons we
still need to pray for forgiveness. But we can do so with the
knowledge that Jesus proclaimed this forgiveness to the people
of his own day. In this sense the petition for forgiveness of sins is
oriented toward the future but rests on the present aspect of the
kingdom of God.

The particular problem that we meet in interpreting this
petition is to determine the relationship between divine and
human forgiveness, since the petition mentions both. Jewish
prayers of the time did not connect God's forgiveness and
human forgiveness.[22] Indeed, Jesus did not often make this
connection in his sayings on forgiveness. But we may look at
two passages in which he spoke of both divine and human forgiveness. We may examine these and ask how they shed light on
the petition for forgiveness in the Lord's Prayer.

In the parable of the unmerciful servant (Matt. 18:23–35),
Jesus spoke of a king who wished to settle accounts with his
servants. One servant owed the king ten thousand talents, or
about ten million dollars. When he could not pay, the king
forgave him the debt. But then this servant refused to forgive
one of his fellow servants who owed him a hundred denarii, or
about twenty dollars. When the king heard what had happened,
he placed the first servant in jail until he should pay all his
debt.

This parable suggests that God's forgiveness precedes human
forgiveness. First God forgives men, and then he expects them
to forgive one another. The parable implies further that human
forgiveness is a reflection of God's forgiveness. Men can, and
should, forgive one another because they have first been forgiven by God. The parable indicates, finally, that God's for-

giveness can become real for men only when they accept it and
make it a part of their lives to such an extent that they are
willing to forgive one another. If they do not forgive one another, they are showing in effect that they have not really accepted the forgiveness that God has offered.

At first sight another passage seems to be inconsistent with
the teachings of this parable. This is the passage that Matthew
has placed after the text of the Lord's Prayer, possibly because
he believed that it explained the meaning of the petition for
forgiveness:

> For if you forgive men their trespasses, your heavenly Father also will
> forgive you; but if you do not forgive men their trespasses, neither will
> your Father forgive your trespasses.
>
> (Matt. 6:14–15; cf. Mark 11:25)

By itself, this passage seems to mean that human forgiveness
precedes God's forgiveness. First men forgive one another, and
then they will receive God's forgiveness. It would appear, in
fact, that human forgiveness makes divine forgiveness possible.
In these ways the passage seems to be inconsistent with the
parable of the unmerciful servant.

We need to remember that the parable makes three points:
(1) God's forgiveness precedes human forgiveness; (2) human
forgiveness is a reflection of God's forgiveness; (3) God's forgiveness can become real for men only when they are willing
to forgive one another. The passage in Matt. 6:14–15 is not
inconsistent with the parable if we think of it as an alternate
statement of the parable's third point. In vivid, forceful language, it says that God's forgiveness can become real for men
only when they receive it and let it change their lives so that
they forgive one another. In this sense there is no inconsistency
between the parable of the unmerciful servant and the saying in
Matt. 6:14–15. In the parable Jesus gives a full explanation of
forgiveness, and in the brief saying he rephrases the third point
of the parable.

The Lord's Prayer reflects the same complete structure of
thought as the parable of the unmerciful servant. The address
abba, "Father," signifies that God accepts men as his children

and brings them into a new relationship with himself. In this way the address itself indicates that divine forgiveness precedes human forgiveness. This new relationship with God enables men to ask for God's forgiveness, and it also enables them to practice forgiveness toward one another. In this sense human forgiveness is a reflection of God's forgiveness. The close connection between the two kinds of forgiveness, and the emphasis on human forgiveness as something that actually takes place, indicate that God's forgiveness can become real only when men accept it and express it by forgiving one another. The parallels between the prayer and the parable are very close, even though the prayer does not have the fuller narrative form of the parable.

This interpretation of the petition for forgiveness agrees with the views that Jesus expressed throughout his ministry. As we saw earlier, Jesus thought of God's forgiveness as a gift that God offers in his own love and mercy toward men. The address *abba* at the beginning of the prayer corresponds to this aspect of forgiveness, for it indicates that God graciously brings men into a new relationship with himself and thus offers them his forgiveness. Jesus also stressed that men must be willing to forgive one another. The emphasis on human forgiveness in the prayer also represents this idea. We saw, finally, that Jesus understood forgiveness within the framework of inaugurated eschatology. The Lord's Prayer also speaks of forgiveness within this context. It invites men to ask that they may receive here and now some of the gifts of the kingdom of God which is already partially present through Jesus' ministry and is still to come in its fullness. Men pray that they may receive forgiveness now, just as they pray that "this day" they may receive their "bread for the morrow."

And lead us not into temptation, but deliver us from evil

In previous petitions we saw that Matthew and Luke sometimes used different Greek words or phrases, and we had to decide which reading represented more accurately the original wording of the prayer. In the present instance Matthew and Luke have the same wording for the petition concerning temptation, and our main problem is to understand what the words mean. We may look first at the expression "lead us not into," and then at the term "temptation." Finally we may look at the request for deliverance from "evil," which appears in Matthew but not in Luke.

Occasionally Christians have been very puzzled by the expression, "lead us not into." It seems to imply that God might indeed lead us into temptation, if we did not ask him not to. But why would God want to lead us into temptation? Would this be consistent with his love and mercy toward men? The author of Psalm 23 writes, "He leads me in paths of righteousness for his name's sake" (23:3). In the Lord's Prayer itself we address God as *abba*, "Father," and we ask him to give us our bread and to forgive our sins. Could the God who does these things have any reason then to lead us into temptation?

Actually the petition does not imply that God would want to lead us into temptation. If we understand it correctly, this problem does not arise. To see why this is so, we need to look at the wording very carefully. We also need to recall that Matthew and Luke give the Lord's Prayer in Greek, while Jesus originally taught it in Aramaic or possibly Hebrew.

The Greek language uses two separate words for the ideas "lead" and "go." Aramaic and Hebrew, however, use only the word "go." When they want to express the idea "lead," they use a special form of "go" that means literally "cause to go." It does not make any difference at this point whether Jesus gave the Lord's Prayer in Aramaic or Hebrew. In either case he would have expressed the idea "lead into" by saying "cause to go into."

Jesus, of course, used the negative "not" when he gave this petition, and our problem is to determine where this negative fits in. Jean Carmignac, developing an earlier suggestion by Johannes Heller, has performed a valuable service by analyzing this type of expression in Hebrew and Aramaic.[23] He shows that the negative "not" can apply either to the idea of "cause" or to the basic meaning of the verb, such as "go." In particular, he calls attention to a number of examples in which the negative applies to the basic meaning of the verb.

Psalm 141 verse 4, for example, uses this type of construction with the verb "incline." The line could be translated, "Do not cause my heart to incline to an evil thing." In this case the problem would arise whether God would want to act in such a way as to incline a person's heart to evil. But the line can also be translated, "Cause my heart not to incline to an evil thing." In this case there is no suggestion at all that God would want to incline anyone toward evil. The person who prays is simply asking for God's help in avoiding anything that is evil.

The Jewish Morning Prayer and Evening Prayer both contain a group of petitions which may be translated literally in this way:

Cause me to go not into the hands of sin, and not into the hands of transgression, and not into the hands of temptation, and not into the hands of dishonor.[24]

The phrase "into the hands of" means "into the power of." Here again, the negative "not" applies to the basic meaning of the verb. The petitions ask God to do something positive, to "cause," with the result that the person does not go into the hands of sin. As in Psalm 141, the person is asking for God's help in avoiding something evil.

This kind of analysis suggests how we should understand the petition, "lead us not into temptation." The verb "lead" means "cause to go," and the negative "not" applies to "go." We could paraphrase the petition, "bring it about that we do not go into temptation," or "help us to avoid temptation." As in the other examples that we have looked at, the person who prays this prayer is asking for God's help in avoiding something evil. When we understand the petition in this way, it does not suggest that God might want to lead men into temptation. Instead, it assumes that God stands ready to help those who call upon him and ask for his assistance.[25]

What then is this "temptation" that we want to avoid? The Jewish Morning Prayer and Evening Prayer both understand the idea in a very general sense, because they associate it with "sin," "transgression," and "dishonor." These Jewish prayers

suggest that "temptation" could refer to any kind of wrongdoing in the course of daily life. According to this interpretation of the word, the petition in the Lord's Prayer would mean
that we ask God to help us avoid anything that is wrong or
sinful.

The structure of the Lord's Prayer offers some support for
this interpretation. The petition for forgiveness of sins comes
right before the petition concerning temptation, and the two
are closely connected by the word "and." First, that is, we pray
that God will forgive the sins that we have already committed,
and then we pray that he will help us avoid any further wrongdoing. When Jesus composed the Lord's Prayer, it is quite possible that he intended to connect the two petitions in this way.

Another interpretation of the word "temptation" is much
more specific. It may refer to the temptation for the followers of
Jesus to deny their faith in times of suffering or persecution.
When Jesus was in Gethsemane, he admonished his disciples,
"Pray that you may not enter into temptation" (Matt. 26:41;
Mark 14:38; Luke 22:40, 46). Jesus knew that his own death
would also place his followers in danger, and he urged them to
pray that they might not give up their faith in this situation.
Apart from the Lord's Prayer itself, this was the only time that
Jesus used the word "temptation" with reference to a situation
that his disciples would face.[26]

We cannot be certain whether Jesus was thinking of his own
death, and the dangerous situation that it would bring, when he
gave the Lord's Prayer. But throughout his ministry he undoubtedly knew that his proclamation of the kingdom of God
could arouse opposition from Jewish authorities and produce a
situation in which his followers would be tempted to fall away.
It is very possible that he had this kind of situation in mind
when he gave the Lord's Prayer and taught his disciples to ask
for God's help in avoiding temptation.

Some interpreters of the Lord's Prayer have understood
temptation in still another way. They believe that it must refer
to the time of testing or tribulation that will come upon the
earth when God achieves his final victory over all the forces of

evil.[27] These interpreters connect the Lord's Prayer with a verse in Revelation, which speaks of "the hour of trial [temptation] which is coming on the whole world" (Rev. 3:10). They believe that the Greek word, which is the same in each case, must refer to the final trial or testing that will come upon the earth when God puts down the forces of evil.

If Jesus thought of the future in this way, then this interpretation of "temptation" cannot be excluded. It does not seem necessary, however, to restrict our understanding of the term to this particular meaning. We have seen that Jesus most probably thought of the kingdom of God as already partially present and still to come in its fullness. To the extent that the kingdom was present, it was already provoking opposition and leading to situations of trial or testing in which the disciples would be tempted to give up their faith. In this sense the petition to avoid temptation would refer to the present as much as the future. It is also important to notice that Jesus himself never used the word "temptation" with the strictly future reference that it has in Rev. 3:10.[28]

We have seen that "temptation" in the Lord's Prayer could refer to wrongdoing in the course of daily life, falling away from faith in times of suffering or persecution, or the final tribulation to come upon the world. There would appear to be more evidence to support the first two interpretations, even if the third cannot be completely excluded. In each case, we may notice, temptation involves the failure to acknowledge the reality of God's rule over the world. It means to act in a way that is inconsistent with God's rule, or to submit to a situation that is opposed to God's rule in the world. In this broad sense "temptation" might include any action or situation that is opposed to the "thou" petitions, which ask God to sanctify his name, establish his kingdom, and do his will in the world.

The Lord's Prayer in Matthew continues with the petition for deliverance from "evil" or from "the evil one." The word "evil" in the Greek text here can be understood as either neuter or masculine. In the first case it would mean the idea or principle of evil, and in the second it would refer to Satan or the devil as "the evil one." In general, the Western, Latin-speaking church has preferred the neuter interpretation, while the Eastern, Greek-speaking church has understood the word in a personal sense as a reference to the devil. We may look first at the evidence for the translation "evil," and then at some factors that support the translation "the evil one."

The writers of the Old Testament often speak of God as the one who delivers his people from evil of some kind. He delivers them, for example, from "all evil" (Gen. 48:16), "all their troubles" (Ps. 34:17), or "those who work evil" (Ps. 59:2). But the Old Testament never refers to the devil as "the evil one."[29] This Old Testament background suggests that Jesus was thinking of "evil" when he gave the Lord's Prayer. He may have used the word to designate the idea or principle of evil, or he may have used it in a general sense to include all the afflictions and troubles that come upon men. But he probably did not use it in a personal sense to mean "the evil one."

In a similar way, Jewish writings speak of God as the one who delivers from various kinds of evil:

Look upon our affliction, and plead our cause, and redeem us for thy name's sake. Blessed art thou, O Lord, Redeemer of Israel.

(Eighteen Benedictions, no. 7)

And may the good impulse rule over me, and may the evil impulse not rule over me; and protect me from an evil occurrence and from evil illnesses; and may evil dreams and evil thoughts not disturb me.

(Evening Prayer)

These examples indicate that Jewish thought applied the idea of evil to a variety of situations that could bring harm to people or lead them into wrongdoing. But there are no examples in which the devil is called "the evil one."[30] Jewish usage, therefore, would also suggest that Jesus meant "evil" in the Lord's Prayer.

It is also important in this connection to look at Jesus' own usage outside the Lord's Prayer. There is some evidence, for instance, that he did speak of "evil" as the principle of evil or something that is evil. He referred to those who "utter all kinds

of evil against you falsely" (Matt. 5:11), and he spoke of the
man who "out of his evil treasure produces evil" (Luke 6:45).
In both cases "evil" is the same word that appears in the Lord's
Prayer, and it is clearly neuter.

It is very uncertain, on the other hand, whether Jesus ever
referred to the devil as "the evil one." There is no example of
this usage in Mark or Luke, and there are only two definite
examples in Matthew. According to Matt. 13:19, Jesus spoke of
"the evil one." The parallels to this verse in Mark and Luke
have "Satan" or "the devil" (Mark 4:15; Luke 8:12), and it is
possible that Jesus actually used one of these words. According
to Matt. 13:38, Jesus also spoke of the devil as "the evil one."
This is a passage, however, that appears only in Matthew.[31]

These considerations all suggest that the petition for deliverance in the Lord's Prayer may well refer to "evil" rather than
"the evil one." There is some evidence, however, that the petition could refer to the devil or Satan. We must also examine
this evidence and weigh it against the factors that support the
interpretation of the word as "evil."

Many Jews in Jesus' day believed in Satan as a supernatural
being who was actively working to gain control over human life
and direct the course of history to his own ends. Together with
his demons or evil spirits, Satan sought to achieve his goals by
causing illness or disease and by enticing men to sin. In this way
Satan and his demons represented a counter-kingdom of evil
that was actively opposed to God's rule in the world. Not all
Jews held this viewpoint, but many accepted it as a way of
understanding the problem of evil in human history and experience.

The accounts in the synoptic Gospels indicate that Jesus
understood the significance of his own ministry in terms of the
struggle between the kingdom of God and the kingdom of
Satan. As he understood this conflict, the kingdom of God was
already gaining the upper hand. He referred to Satan when he
said that it was necessary to bind "the strong man" (Mark
3:27). He cast out demons as a sign that the kingdom of God
had come (Matt. 12:28; Luke 11:20). He prayed that Simon

Peter might have the strength to keep his faith when Satan tempted him to deny it (Luke 22:31–32). He spoke a number of times of "the devil" or "Satan."[32] It seems clear, therefore, that Jesus accepted the contemporary Jewish view of Satan as a personal being. In this sense it is possible that he did speak of Satan as "the evil one."

We may also notice that some later New Testament writers referred to Satan as "the evil one."[33] The author of the first letter of John, for example, writes, "I am writing to you, young men, because you have overcome the evil one" (1 John 2:13). We cannot assume that this expression necessarily represents Jesus' own usage, since the actual evidence for his use of the phrase is very limited. It is possible, however, that the later use of the phrase rests on a tradition that goes back to Jesus himself. In this sense the later New Testament usage could give some support to the view that Jesus spoke of Satan as "the evil one."

The evidence on the whole seems to indicate that the petition for deliverance refers to "evil" rather than "the evil one." The most important consideration is that Jesus seldom, if ever, referred to Satan as "the evil one." We must also notice that there is some uncertainty whether Jesus himself included this petition when he gave the Lord's Prayer. Matthew has the petition, but Luke's version of the Lord's Prayer omits it. There would seem to be no adequate reason to explain why Luke would want to omit the petition if he knew of it as part of the prayer.

The "we" petitions as a group are closely related to the "thou" petitions within the structure of the Lord's Prayer. In the "thou" petitions the disciples of Jesus ask God to act in the world and make known his salvation. Then in the "we" petitions they ask God to meet their own needs in the present time as they seek to live within God's kingdom and look forward to its fulfillment. They pray that they may receive, here and now the gifts of the new time of salvation that God is already inaugurating. In this way the "thou" petitions refer to God's own actions in the world, and the "we" petitions refer to the need of the disciples as they seek to respond to God's actions and live within his kingdom.

Chapter Five

The Doxology

For thine is the kingdom and the power and the glory forever. Amen.

(Matt. 6:13)

A doxology is an ascription of praise to God. As praise, it is closely related to gratitude, trust, and hope. In a doxology the people praise God for having certain characteristics or qualities. They praise him in a mood of thankfulness that he has made these qualities known to them. At the same time they are expressing a sense of trust in God, for they believe that he will continue to show these qualities. This sense of trust, in turn, gives them confidence and hope for the future. In this way the expression of praise to God is also an expression of gratitude, trust, and hope.

The doxology appears at the close of the Lord's Prayer in some early manuscripts and translations of Matthew, but not in others. It does not appear in connection with Luke's version of the prayer. The *Didache* gives a shorter form of the doxology: "For thine is the power and the glory forever." Throughout Christian history the doxology has been included in some translations of Matthew's version of the prayer, but it has been omitted from others. It was included, for example, in Luther's Bible and in the King James translation. It was omitted, on the other hand, from the Latin Vulgate, the German Bibles before Luther, and the New Testaments of Wycliffe, Tyndale, and Coverdale.[1]

The early textual evidence suggests that Jesus himself did not include the doxology when he gave the Lord's Prayer. There is reason to believe, on the other hand, that he expected the disciples to conclude the prayer in some way such as this. It was a Jewish principle that a prayer had to end "with something good."[2] Jesus, that is, would not have wanted the prayer to end with a word like "temptation" or "evil." He undoubtedly assumed that the disciples themselves would conclude the prayer with an appropriate expression of praise to God.

In composing the doxology, the disciples drew on their rich liturgical heritage in the Old Testament and Judaism. According to the first book of Chronicles, for example, King David began a prayer with a doxology that is somewhat similar to the doxology in the Lord's Prayer, although much longer:

Blessed art thou, O Lord, the God of Israel our father, for ever and ever. Thine, O Lord, is the greatness, and the power, and the glory, and the victory, and the majesty; for all that is in the heavens and in the earth is thine; thine is the kingdom, O Lord, and thou art exalted as head above all. Both riches and honor come from thee, and thou rulest over all. In thy hand are power and might; and in thy hand it is to make great and to give strength to all. And now we thank thee, our God, and praise thy glorious name.

(1 Chron. 29:10–13)

Judaism, too, was rich in material of this kind. Each section of the Eighteen Benedictions ended with a brief doxology. The Morning Prayer and the Evening Prayer each ended with a doxology. The Kaddish closed with a doxology that was almost as long as the prayer itself. Part of this doxology was spoken in unison by the congregation and the leader, and part was spoken by the leader with the congregation saying "amen" as a response. Translations of these four prayers are given in the appendix to this book.

The worship services of the Jerusalem temple also included a doxology that is somewhat similar to the one in the Lord's Prayer: "Blessed be the name of his glorious kingdom for ever and ever." During the morning worship service the people gave this doxology as a response to the prayer *Ahaba Rabba*, "Great Love." Later in the service the people gave the doxology again in response to the "Aaronic blessing" of Num. 6:24–26.[3] Since the Jersualem temple was still standing during Jesus' lifetime and for about forty years after his death, it is very possible that the early Christians were familiar with this doxology from the temple worship.

None of these doxologies is exactly the same as the one in the

Lord's Prayer. The doxology in 1 Chron. 29:10–13 has the words "kingdom," "power," and "glory," but it gives them in a different order from the Lord's Prayer. This doxology also comes at the beginning of the prayer rather than at the end. The doxology in the Evening Prayer mentions God's "glory," and the temple doxology refers to his "kingdom." Although these doxologies do not correspond exactly to the one in the Lord's Prayer, they illustrate the kind of material that the disciples of Jesus or the early Christians could draw on in composing a doxology of their own.

In the doxology of the Lord's Prayer, the word "kingdom" probably refers to God's eternal kingship over his world. This is the same meaning that the term has in the doxology of 1 Chron. 29:10–13 and in the temple doxology. This rather general meaning of "kingdom" was especially characteristic of Jewish thought, even though some of the Jews also used the word in an eschatological sense.

Jesus, on the other hand, usually used the word in an eschatological sense to designate the new time of salvation that God was bringing. He used it this way in the second petition of the Lord's Prayer, "Thy kingdom come." Jesus evidently accepted the idea that God was eternally king over his world, but he put his own emphasis on the thought that God was now acting decisively to assert his kingship and establish it in the world.

It is very likely, therefore, that the "kingdom" of God has different meanings in the second petition and in the doxology of the Lord's Prayer. We can understand this difference if we assume that Jesus himself gave the second petition, while his followers were responsible for adding the doxology. In the second petition Jesus spoke of God's kingdom in an eschatological sense. In the doxology his followers used the term in the more general sense that was characteristic of Judaism, since they were influenced at this point by the doxologies of Jewish prayers and liturgy.

In a similar way it is likely that Jesus' followers included the words "power" and "glory" because they were familiar with the use of these terms in the Old Testament and Judaism. It is interesting, for example, that these words appear along with "kingdom" in one of the psalms of praise in the Old Testament:

> All thy works shall give thanks to thee, O Lord,
>   and all thy saints shall bless thee!
> They shall speak of the glory of thy kingdom,
>   and tell of thy power,
> to make known to the sons of men thy mighty deeds,
>   and the glorious splendor of thy kingdom.
> Thy kingdom is an everlasting kingdom,
>   and thy dominion endures throughout all generations.
> (Ps. 145:10–13)

God's "power" in this passage refers especially to his working in history on behalf of his covenant people (cf. Deut. 3:24; Josh. 4:23–24; Ps. 77:14–15). Elsewhere in the Old Testament the word signifies God's power in creating and sustaining the world (cf. Isa. 40:26; Jer. 27:5; 32:17). Both of these meanings continued in later Jewish thought.[4] When the followers of Jesus included this word in the doxology of the Lord's Prayer, it is entirely possible that they were thinking of God's power as it is manifested in history and also in the creation of the world.

The term "glory" reflects an Old Testament word that originally meant "heaviness" or "weight." God's glory, therefore, is his "importance" or "honor" (cf. Ps. 24:8; 138:5). When men give glory to God, they are recognizing the importance of his nature and character as God (cf. Jer. 13:16; Ps. 29:1–2; 96:7–8; 115:1). The glory of God is also the "splendor" or "radiance" of his presence when he manifests himself to his people (cf. Exod. 16:10; 40:34). These various meanings of God's glory as "honor," "importance," and "splendor" lived on in Judaism.[5] The reference to God's glory in the doxology suggests that God has these qualities in a unique way, which no other can share.

The doxology of the Lord's Prayer has a "Jewish" character in the sense that the words "kingdom," "power," and "glory" seem to have the same meaning that they usually have in the Old Testament and Judaism. We would expect this to be the case if the followers of Jesus composed the doxology by drawing on materials that they were acquainted with in the Old Testament and Judaism. It was natural that they would express their praise and thanksgiving to God in terms that reflect their own religious heritage.

At the same time, the doxology is an appropriate ending to the Lord's Prayer itself. Within the context of the prayer, it expresses gratitude to God for bringing men into a new relationship with himself so that they can address him as *abba*, "Father." It also expresses confidence that God will do what the "thou" petitions and the "we" petitions ask him to do. In this way the doxology refers to every part of the prayer. It is a fitting conclusion to the prayer because it reflects a sense of heartfelt trust that God will hear and answer the prayer.

The word "amen" was usually added at the close of the doxology in early manuscripts and translations of the Lord's Prayer.[6] Literally this word meant "firm," "constant," or "valid." As a response to something that someone else said, it meant "may it be so." When a person said "amen" to another person's prayer, he was indicating that he shared in it and was making it his own. Occasionally in Judaism a person would also end his own prayer with "amen."[7]

In Judaism the use of "amen" was especially characteristic of synagogue worship. The congregation gave this response to the phrases of thanksgiving that the worship leader used in connection with prayers or other parts of the service.[8] In a similar way the "amen" at the end of the Lord's Prayer probably indicates that the early Christians used the prayer in their own worship services. They regarded the Lord's Prayer as a central part of their corporate worship, even though individual Christians could also use the prayer privately in the course of their daily lives.

The *Didache* also suggests that the Lord's Prayer was both a corporate and an individual prayer. When it gives the prayers of thanksgiving that are offered during and after the celebration of the Lord's Supper, it concludes them with the words, "For thine is the power and the glory forever" (9:4; 10:5). This is the same doxology that appears at the end of the Lord's Prayer in the *Didache*, and it suggests that the Lord's Prayer itself was used at some point in the celebration of the Lord's Supper. On the other hand, the *Didache* also instructs Christians to pray the Lord's Prayer three times a day (8:3). This regulation indicates that the prayer was also used privately in the course of daily life.

Throughout history, Christians have used the Lord's Prayer in corporate services of worship and in their own private prayers as individuals. As the *Didache* indicates, each way of using the prayer goes back as early as the first century. The Lord's Prayer is appropriate for public worship because it expresses the faith of all Christians as they call upon God to complete his work of salvation and satisfy their needs in the present time. The prayer is also appropriate for private use because every individual Christian shares in the hopes and aspirations of the community. When the individual person prays the Lord's Prayer, he is joining himself with all other Christians, throughout the world and throughout the centuries, who have called upon God in prayer and addressed him as *abba*, "Father."

Chapter Six

The Lord's Prayer and Christian Faith

Our main purpose in this book has been to understand the Lord's Prayer itself. We have analyzed the structure of the prayer and examined the meaning of the various words and phrases that Jesus used in the prayer. In some instances, as we have seen, different interpretations are possible, so that we cannot always be certain exactly what Jesus meant. But this kind of study can help us to appreciate the spiritual value of the prayer. The more clearly we can understand its meaning, the more we can appreciate its significance for Jesus' first disciples and for all of his followers throughout the centuries of Christian history.

In this final chapter we may broaden the scope of our inquiry by looking at the relationship between the Lord's Prayer and Christian faith. In one sense it is clear that this relationship is very close. The Lord's Prayer is the only prayer that Jesus gave to his followers, and for this reason alone it has had a central place in Christian life and thought. It also expresses a number of ideas that have always been important in Christianity, such as the fatherhood of God, the kingdom of God, divine and human forgiveness, and preservation from temptation. The early church father, Tertullian, must have been thinking of the prayer in this way when he described it as a "summary of the whole gospel" (*breviarium totius evangelii*).

We should also notice, on the other hand, that the Lord's Prayer makes no direct reference to some of the central beliefs of Christian faith. It does not speak of Jesus as Lord, Christ, or Savior. It does not refer to the significance of Jesus' life, death, or Resurrection. It has no explicit reference to other ideas that have usually been important for Christians, such as their concern for peace and justice in the world, their intercessory prayer for others, their role as the new people of God, or their hope for everlasting life. In ways such as these it might seem that the Lord's Prayer leaves out many beliefs or ideas that have traditionally been very important in Christianity.

There are several factors that we can take into consideration as we try to assess the relationship between the Lord's Prayer and Christian faith. We need to remember, for instance, that Jesus probably intended the Lord's Prayer as a model for prayer. He assumed that his followers might make some additions or expansions, and he also assumed that they would compose other prayers that would be appropriate for specific needs or situations. This does not detract from the central importance of the Lord's Prayer. But it does suggest that Christians also find it meaningful to use other prayers as they are appropriate for specific occasions.

We may also notice that the Lord's Prayer itself suggests some themes of Christian faith, even though it does not state them explicitly or develop them fully. The Lord's Prayer, for instance, has no direct reference to Jesus. But it begins by addressing God as *abba*, "Father." Jesus used this word as an expression of his own close relationship with God, and then he instructed his disciples to use it as a way of addressing their heavenly Father. In this way the term *abba* refers implicitly to Jesus' own status as the Son of God. At the same time it refers to the role of the disciples as children of God and the nucleus of a new people of God, who already receive some of the gifts of the new time of salvation and seek to proclaim their Father's rule in the world.

The Lord's Prayer has no direct reference to intercessory prayer, Christian life in the world, or the hope for everlasting life. But there is an intercessory aspect, as we have seen, to the "thou" petitions. When Christians pray that God may sanctify his name and establish his kingdom, they are asking him to act in a way that will ultimately affect the whole world. In this sense they are praying on behalf of other people, as well as themselves. When they work for peace and justice in the world, they are responding to God's rule over the world and helping to implement it in concrete situations. When they look forward to the future, they know that God has already begun to establish a new time of salvation that will ultimately include everlasting life in his presence.

In ways such as these the Lord's Prayer suggests or implies a number of ideas that Christians have stated more explicitly as they seek to formulate the meaning of their faith. We must be careful to recognize that the Lord's Prayer itself is a prayer rather than a complete summary of Christian beliefs. We can, on the other hand, notice how the various words and phrases in the Lord's Prayer foreshadow certain beliefs about God, Jesus, and Christian life that Christians have regarded as central to their faith.

A final factor of significance in this connection is the central importance of the Resurrection of Jesus. This helped the early Christians to understand, more clearly than before, that Jesus was indeed Lord, Christ, and Son of God (cf. Acts 2:36; Rom. 1:4). Because they believed in Jesus as the risen Lord, they could look back on his earthly ministry and see it in a new perspective. They gained a new appreciation of his earthly ministry because they realized now that the earthly Jesus and the risen Lord were the same person. From this perspective they wrote the New Testament Gospels as a way of preserving their recollections of Jesus' teachings and activities during his earthly ministry.

The identity between the earthly Jesus and the risen Lord does not mean that the Lord's Prayer, for example, must contain a reference to Jesus' Resurrection. There is no reason to think that it does. But it does mean that the Lord's Prayer, like Jesus' other teachings and activities, can be understood most fully in light of faith in Jesus as the risen Lord. The one who gave the prayer is also the risen Lord, and the risen Lord is the one who lived and taught among men. For Christians throughout the centuries, this continuity of personal identity between the earthly Jesus and the risen Lord has meant that praying the Lord's Prayer is also an expression of faith in Jesus as the risen Lord.

Jewish Prayers in Jesus' Time

The following pages give four Jewish prayers that very possibly existed in Jesus' day. It is not certain exactly when the prayers first came into use, because they were written down in a later period. The Kaddish and the Eighteen Benedictions are given here in early forms rather than the longer forms that came into general usage later. Scholars believe that in their early forms these two prayers, as well as the Morning Prayer and the Evening Prayer, could well go back to Jesus' own time.[1]

These four prayers are especially important because they offer approximate parallels to sections of the Lord's Prayer. The Kaddish corresponds to the "thou" petitions in the sense that it mentions God's name, kingdom, and will. The Eighteen Benedictions are somewhat similar to the first two "we" petitions in referring to the fruits of the earth (no. 9) and to forgiveness (no. 6). The Morning Prayer and the Evening Prayer correspond to the last two "we" petitions when they ask God's help in avoiding various kinds of temptation and evil. All four prayers include doxologies, or ascriptions of praise to God.

The prayers illustrate the kind of material that Jesus was familiar with in the Judaism of his time, even though he did not always use their terms and ideas in exactly the same way when he composed the Lord's Prayer. For the modern reader these prayers also offer an insight into the spiritual depth and vitality of first century Judaism.

The Kaddish[2]

Leader:
>   Magnified and sanctified be his great name in the world,
>   which he created according to his will;

and may he establish his kingdom in your lifetime
and in your days and in the lifetime of all the house
of Israel, quickly and soon.
And say: Amen.

Congregation and Leader:
May his great name be blessed
forever and forever and ever.

Leader:
Exalted above all praises and songs,
words of glory and consolation,
which are spoken in the world.
And say: Amen.

The Eighteen Benedictions[3]

1. Blessed art thou, O Lord, God of Abraham, God of Isaac,
and God of Jacob, the most high God, Creator of heaven
and earth, our Shield and the Shield of our fathers. Blessed
art thou, O Lord, Shield of Abraham.

2. Thou art mighty and strong, and thou livest forever. Thou
raisest the dead, sustainest the living, and givest life to the
dead. Blessed art thou, O Lord, who givest life to the dead.

3. Holy art thou, and awesome is thy name, and there is no
God besides thee. Blessed art thou, O Lord, the holy God.

4. Bestow upon us, our Father, knowledge from thee and
discernment and understanding from thy law. Blessed art
thou, O Lord, who bestowest knowledge.

5. Restore us, O Lord, to thee, that we may turn back. Renew
our days as in times past. Blessed art thou, O Lord, who
delightest in repentance.

6. Forgive us, our Father, for we have sinned against thee; blot out our transgressions from before thine eyes. Blessed art thou, O Lord, who forgivest much.

7. Look upon our affliction, and plead our cause, and redeem us for thy name's sake. Blessed art thou, O Lord, Redeemer of Israel.

8. Heal us, O Lord our God, from the pain of our hearts, and bring healing for our afflictions. Blessed art thou, who healest the sick of thy people Israel.

9. Bless this year unto us, O Lord our God, and fill the world with the treasures of thy goodness. Blessed art thou, O Lord, who blessest the years.

10. Sound the great horn for our freedom, and raise up a banner to gather our exiles. Blessed art thou, O Lord, who gatherest the dispersed of thy people Israel.

11. Restore our judges as in times past and our counsellors as at the beginning, and be King over us, thou alone. Blessed art thou, O Lord, who lovest justice.

12. For the rebellious may there be no hope, and the dominion of arrogance mayest thou quickly blot out. Blessed art thou, O Lord, who humblest the arrogant.

13. May thy mercy pour down upon the proselytes of righteousness, and give us a good reward with those who do thy will. Blessed art thou, O Lord, the trust of the righteous.

14. Have mercy, O Lord our God, on Jerusalem thy city, and on Zion the habitation of thy glory, and on the kingdom of the house of David, the Anointed One of thy righteousness. Blessed art thou, O Lord, the God of David, who buildest Jerusalem.

15. Hear our prayer, O Lord our God, for thou art a gracious and merciful God. Blessed art thou, O Lord, who hearest prayer.

16. May it please the Lord our God to dwell in Zion, that thy servants may serve thee in Jerusalem. Blessed art thou, O Lord, that we may serve thee in fear.

17. We thank thee, O Lord our God, for every good thing and for the love which thou hast shown to us. Blessed art thou, O Lord, and to thee be thanks.

18. Grant thy peace to thy people Israel and bless all of us together. Blessed art thou, O Lord, who bringest peace.

The Morning Prayer[4]

Blessed be he who removes sleep from my eyes and slumber from my lids.

And may it please thee, Eternal One, my God, to guide my feet in thy law, and let me cling to thy law, and let me cling to thy commandments.

And bring me not into the hands of sin, or into the hands of transgression, or into the hands of temptation, or into the hands of dishonor; and humble my spirit, to submit to thee.

And keep me far from an evil man and from an evil companion; and let me cling to the good impulse and to a good companion in this world.

And grant me today and every day favor and grace and mercy in thine eyes and in the eyes of everyone who sees me; and bestow kindness upon me.

Blessed art thou, Eternal One, who bestowest kindness upon thy people Israel.

The Evening Prayer[5]

He who lowers the bonds of sleep upon my eyes and slumber upon my lids, and grants light to the eye:

May it please thee, Eternal One, my God, to let me lie down in peace, and give me my share in your law.

And guide my foot to fulfill a commandment, and guide my foot not to commit a transgression.

And bring me not into the hands of sin, or into the hands of transgression, or into the hands of temptation, or into the hands of dishonor.

And may the good impulse rule over me, and may the evil impulse not rule over me.

And protect me from an evil occurrence and from evil illnesses; and may evil dreams and evil thoughts not disturb me.

And may my bed be pure before thee; and enlighten my eyes, lest I sleep the sleep of death.

Blessed art thou, Eternal One, who givest light to the whole world by thy glory.

NOTES

AND

INDEXES

Notes

NOTES TO PAGES 1–22

1. Some early manuscripts and translations of the prayer reflect a tendency to assimilate Luke's form to Matthew's, evidently because Matthew's form was used more widely. This process was virtually complete in the Koine group of manuscripts, which represented the type of text used for the King James translation. The process of assimilation was already beginning in the Old Latin and Old Syriac translations and in Codex Sinaiticus. The short Lukan text appeared in early sources such as the Vulgate, Codex Vaticanus (fourth century), and Bodmer Papyrus p^{75} (second or third century). The fragment of the prayer in the Antinoopolis papyri (third century) contains parts of the third, fourth, and fifth petitions of Matthew's version, although the word "debt" is in the singular. On this fragment cf. E. Bammel, "A New Text of the Lord's Prayer," *Expository Times* 73 (Oct. 1961–Sept. 1962):54.

2. The word *Didache* means "Teaching"; the full title is *The Teaching of the Twelve Apostles*. For a discussion of the writing and a summary of critical problems cf. M. H. Shepherd, Jr., "Didache," in George A. Buttrick, ed., *The Interpreter's Dictionary of the Bible*, 4 vols. (New York: Abingdon Press, 1962), 1:841–43.

3. Cf. I. Abrahams, *Studies in Pharisaism and the Gospels*, Second Series (Cambridge: The University Press, 1924), p. 104.

4. For an analysis of the setting of the Lord's Prayer in Matthew and Luke, to which the present discussion is indebted, cf. J. Jeremias, *The Lord's Prayer* (Philadelphia: Fortress Press, 1964), pp. 8–10.

5. For the daily use of the Eighteen Benedictions, also known as the Tephillah (i.e., the "prayer"), cf. Berakoth 4.1. A convenient source of the reference is H. Danby, *The Mishnah* (Oxford: Oxford University Press, 1933), p. 5.

6. For a Hebrew reconstruction cf. J. Carmignac, *Recherches sur le "Notre Père,"* (Paris: Letouzey & Ané, 1969), p. 396. Aramaic reconstructions are available in Jeremias, *The Lord's Prayer*, p. 15; and E. Lohmeyer, *Our Father* (New York: Harper & Row, 1965), pp. 27–29. All of these reconstructions show the characteristics noted above, except that some use the possessive "our" less freely than the Greek text. On the question of rhyme within these two sections of the Lord's Prayer cf. B. Noack, *Om Fadervor* (Copenhagen: G. E. C. Gad, 1969), pp. 23–24; and K. G. Kuhn, *Achtzehngebet und Vaterunser und der Reim* (Tübingen: J. C. B. Mohr, 1950), pp. 30–40.

7. Cf. S. Van Tilborg, "A Form-Criticism of the Lord's Prayer," *Novum Testamentum* 14 (1972):94–105. For a similar view that derives the prayer from materials in Mark, cf. M. D. Goulder, "The Composition of the Lord's Prayer," *The Journal of Theological Studies*, New Series 14 (1963):32–45. B. Noack points out that the explicit contrast between Jesus' will and God's will is emphasized in the Gethsemane accounts but is absent from the Lord's Prayer. This makes it less likely that the third petition of the prayer is derived from the Gethsemane account. Cf. Noack, *Om Fadervor*, pp. 70–71.

8. This method is usually called the *criterion of dissimilarity*. For the method, and others that supplement it, see N. Perrin, *Rediscovering the Teaching of Jesus* (New York: Harper & Row, 1967), pp. 39–47.

9. See especially Jeremias, *The Lord's Prayer*, pp. 10–15; Jeremias regards Luke's form as original, although in some instances he prefers Matthew's wording. Other advocates of Lukan priority include R. E. Brown, "The Pater Noster as an Eschatological Prayer," in *New Testament Essays* (Milwaukee: The Bruce Publishing Company, 1965), pp. 217–53, especially pp. 218–20; E. von Dobschütz, "The Lord's Prayer," *Harvard Theological Review* 7 (1914):293–321, especially pp. 299–300; and Kuhn, *Achtzehngebet und Vaterunser und der Reim*, p. 39.

10. For these arguments cf. E. F. Scott, *The Lord's Prayer* (New York: Charles Scribner's Sons, 1951), pp. 27–30 and Carmignac, *Recherches sur le "Notre Père,"* pp. 23–26. Both writers regard Matthew's form of the prayer as original. Their arguments are rephrased here, but the first five are found in Scott, and the first, third, fourth, and sixth in Carmignac.

11. Cf. Carmignac, *Recherches sur le "Notre Père,"* pp. 25, 27, 383–86, 396.

12. For examples of such incantations see Sherman E. Johnson, "Matthew," in George A. Buttrick, ed., *The Interpreter's Bible*, vol. 7, *General Articles, Matthew, Mark* (New York: Abingdon-Cokesbury Press, 1951), p. 308.

13. This is the view of P. Fiebig, *Das Vaterunser* (Gütersloh: C. Bertelsmann, 1927), especially pp. 18–28, 45–46. Fiebig is especially concerned to point out parallels between the Lord's Prayer and Jewish prayers of the time. He believes that Jesus himself expanded the short form of the prayer, mainly on the basis of phrases in the Kaddish and the Morning and Evening Prayers. This view is not impossible, but it makes Jesus himself responsible for the differences between the two versions without explaining satisfactorily why he would modify his own prayer.

14. An important recent study is Günther Schwarz, "Matthäus V. 9–13/ Lukas XI. 2–4: Emendation und Rückübersetzung," *New Testament Studies* 15 (1968–69):233–47. On the basis of certain criteria, especially two-stress lines, end rhyme, and synonymous parallelism, Schwarz believes that Jesus gave the following prayer: "Father: Hallowed be thy name; Thy kingdom come; Thy will be done; Give us our bread; And forgive us our debts; And deliver us from our temptation." Thus in general Matthew expanded, and Luke abridged, the original prayer. Although this theory is ingenious, it has several weaknesses: it applies stylistic criteria

too rigidly, it fails to explain why the rare word *epiousios* would have entered the text, and it rather artificially produces a single petition from the ones concerning temptation and evil.

15. Thus Noack, *Om Fadervor*, pp. 19, 25. Noack also stresses that the content and meaning of the prayer are the same in either case.

16. Ezra 4:8–6:18; 7:12–26; Dan. 2:4b–7:28. The gloss in Jer. 10:11 is also in Aramaic.

17. Carmignac, *Recherches sur le "Notre Père*," pp. 30–31.

18. Ibid., pp. 32–33.

19. Translations of these four prayers, with references, are given in the appendix.

20. Sotah 7, 1 (in Danby, *The Mishnah*, p. 300).

21. The Shema consists of Deut. 6:4–9; 11:13–21; Num. 15:37–41. The word "shema" means "hear!" Being the first word of Deut. 6:4, it supplies the name for the group of passages.

22. Sotah 7, 1 (in Danby, The *Mishnah*, p. 300).

23. On Jewish worship services cf. Hermann L. Strack and Paul Billerbeck, *Kommentar zum Neuen Testament aus Talmud und Midrasch*, 5 vols. (Munich: C. H. Beck, 1922–56), 4 (pt. 1): 153–249 (hereafter cited as Strack/Billerbeck); also Paul Billerbeck, "Ein Tempelgottesdienst in Jesu Tagen," *Zeitschrift für die neutestamentliche Wissenschaft* 55 (1964): 1–17; "Ein Synagogengottesdienst in Jesu Tagen," *Zeitschrift für die neutestamentliche Wissenschaft* 55 (1964): 143–61.

24. Sotah 7, 2 (in Danby, *The Mishnah*, p. 300).

25. When Jesus prays to God as "Father" or "My Father," several forms of the Greek word appear in the synoptic Gospels: the vocative alone (Matt. 11:25; Luke 10:21; 11:2; 22:42; 23:34, 46); the vocative with possessive pronoun (Matt. 6:9; 26:39, 42); the arthrous nominative used as a vocative (Matt. 11:26; Mark 14:36; Luke 10:21). The best explanation for this puzzling variety of forms is that the Aramaic term *abba* underlies them all, since *abba* was used rather freely for "father," "my father," and even "our father." Cf. Gerhard Kittel and Gerhard Friedrich, eds., *Theological Dictionary of the New Testament*, 9 vols. (Grand Rapids: Wm. B. Eerdmans, 1964–73), 1:5–6; also ibid. 5:985. The view that Jesus used *abba* in his own prayers is also supported by W. Marchel, *Abba, Père! La Prière du Christ et des Chrétiens* (Rome: Biblical Institute Press, 1971), pp. 124–38.

26. Cf. especially Jeremias, *The Lord's Prayer*, pp. 17–21; also idem, *"Abba,"* in *The Prayers of Jesus* (Naperville, Ill.: Alec R. Allenson, 1967), pp. 54–65.

27. Jeremias gives the following references in the Mishnah for *abba* in the sense of "our father": Shebuoth 7, 7, Baba Bathra 9, 3 (in Danby, *The Mishnah*, pp. 420, 378). For these and additional references in the Tosephta cf. Jeremias, *"Abba,"* p. 59, n. 37.

28. For an alternative explanation of the early Christian use of *abba* cf. Marchel, *Abba, Père! La Prière du Christ et des Chrétiens*, pp. 170–89.

Marchel believes that Jesus used the word *abba* in his own prayers but did not instruct his disciples to use it; the early Christians began to use it only as they became more aware of their union with Christ as the risen Lord. But Jesus' understanding of the kingdom of God would seem to provide the context in which he could give his disciples the privilege of addressing God by the same term that he used. As the kingdom was already partially present in Jesus' ministry, men were already being brought into a new relationship with God and could begin, therefore, to address him as *abba*.

29. Cf. Kittel and Friedrich, *Theological Dictionary of the New Testament*, 5:562–65.

30. The root *chwb* is not frequent in the Old Testament; the Piel of the verb occurs in Dan. 1:10, and the noun in Ezek. 18:7. The word *neshi*, "debt," occurs only in 2 Kings 4:7. A related word, *mashsha'*, "debt," occurs in Neh. 5:7, 10, and 10:32 (English 10:31). The similar term *mashsha'a*, "loan," occurs in Deut. 24:10; Prov. 22:26; and possibly Neh. 5:11. The various Hebrew terms for sin reflect ideas other than "debt"; *pesha'* is rebellion against God, *chatta't* is missing the mark, and *'awon* is intentional deviation from the right way.

NOTES TO PAGES 23–56

1. The Greek of the Gospels uses the expressions "Father (who art, is) in heaven" and "heavenly Father." These are equivalent in meaning, since they represent different ways of rendering Hebrew and Aramaic phrases that mean literally "Father who in the heavens."

2. Matt. 5:16, 45, 48; 6:1, 14, 26, 32; 7:11, 21; 10:32, 33; 12:50; 15:13; 16:17; 18:10, 14, 19, 35; 23:9. Mark 11:25. Luke 11:13. Of the nineteen verses in Matthew, nine have parallel verses in Luke (cf. Luke 6:35, 36; 8:21; 11:13; 12:8, 9, 24, 30; 15:7). Only one of these verses in Luke (11:13) speaks of God as "Father in heaven." The other eight speak simply of "Father" or use other expressions altogether.

3. Cf. J. Jeremias, *"Abba,"* in *The Prayers of Jesus* (Naperville, Ill.: Alec R. Allenson, 1967), p. 16, especially n. 8.

4. Seder Eliyyahu Rabba 28 (149), in Strack/Billerbeck, 1:394.

5. Matt. 11:25, 26; 26:39, 42; Mark 14:36; Luke 10:21 (twice); 22:42; 23:34, 46.

6. Matt. 11:25, 26; Luke 10:21 (twice).

7. Matt. 26:39, 42; Mark 14:36; Luke 22:42.

8. Luke 23:34.

9. Luke 23:46.

10. Sota 9, 15, in Strack/Billerbeck, 1:394; cf. also Targ. Esth. 5, 14, in ibid., p. 396.

11. Targ. Jerush. I. Ex. 1:19 in ibid., p. 396.

12. Aboth 5, 20 in ibid., p. 395.

13. Targ. Jerush. I. Lev. 22:28 in ibid., p. 395.

14. Cf. Gerhard Kittel and Gerhard Friedrich, eds., *Theological Dictionary of the New Testament*, 9 vols. (Grand Rapids: Wm. B. Eerdmans, 1964–73), 5:980.

15. Seder Eliyyahu Rabba 21 end, in Strack/Billerbeck, 1:410.

16. From "A Hymn to Amon-Re," in J. B. Pritchard, ed., *Ancient Near Eastern Texts*, 2d ed. (Princeton: Princeton University Press, 1955), pp. 365–67.

17. From "The Asiatic Campaigning of Amen-hotep II," in ibid., p. 246. The selections in Pritchard give numerous examples of the sun-god (Amon-Re, or Amon or Re individually) as father of the pharaoh; cf. especially pp. 231–63. Occasionally other gods are mentioned as father of the pharaoh; cf. pp. 248–58, 329, 449.

18. From W. Marchel, *Abba, Père! La Prière du Christ et des Chrétiens* (Rome: Biblical Institute Press, 1971), p. 37. Marchel quotes from P. Gilbert, *La poésie égyptienne* (Brussels, 1943), pp. 19ff.

19. Cf. Pritchard, *Ancient Near Eastern Texts*, pp. 235, 242.

20. Marchel, *Abba, Père! La Prière du Christ et des Chrétiens*, p. 37. Marchel refers to E. Drioton, "Une nouvelle source d'information sur la religion égyptienne," in *La Revue du Caire*, 2 (1951): 13.

21. Pritchard, *Ancient Near Eastern Texts*, pp. 385–86.

22. Ibid., pp. 98, 459, 462, 463.

23. Ibid., p. 391.

24. Cf. Marchel, *Abba, Père! La Prière du Christ et des Chrétiens*, p. 31.

25. E.g., Homer *Iliad* 1. 544; 4. 68; 5. 426; 8. 49, 132; 11. 182; 15. 12, 47; 16. 458; 20. 56; 22. 167; 24. 103. Homer *Odyssey* 1. 28.

26. Homer *Iliad* 3. 320–23 (translated by A. T. Murray in the *Loeb Classical Library* [Cambridge, Mass.: Harvard University Press, 1965], p. 141). For other examples of the address "Father Zeus" cf. *Iliad* 1. 503; 3. 276, 365; 7. 179, 202; 15. 372; 17. 645; 24. 308.

27. *Helen* 11. 1441–45 (translated by A. S. Way in the *Loeb Classical Library* [Cambridge, Mass.: Harvard University Press, 1959], p. 591). For other references to Zeus as Father cf. Pindar *Nemean Odes* 8, 1. 35; 9, 1. 31; *Isthmian Odes* 6, 1. 42; *Pythian Odes* 4, 1. 194; Sophocles *Trachiniae* 1. 275; Aristophanes *The Acharnians* 1. 224.

28. Plato *Republic* 6. 506E.

29. Ibid., 7. 517C. The translation is slightly revised from that of P. Shorey in the *Loeb Classical Library* (Cambridge, Mass.: Harvard University Press, 1942), p. 131.

30. Plato *Timaeus* 28C; cf. 37C, 41A.

31. From Marchel, *Abba, Père! La Prière du Christ et des Chrétiens*, p. 64.

32. Cf. Epictetus *Discourses* 1. 3. 1, 6. 40, 9. 22–25, 19. 9; 2. 8. 18, 14. 23–29.

33. Cf. especially ibid., 2. 8. 9–23.

34. Cf. Kittel and Friedrich, *Theological Dictionary of the New Testament,* 5:953–54.

35. Ibid., p. 951.

36. Cf. Book of Jubilees 1:13–15; 15:34; 21:21–23; 22:16–23; 23:23–24.

37. The Testaments of the Twelve Patriarchs; cf. especially Levi 2:11; 4:4; 5:7; 8:14; 14:4; 18:9; Simeon 6:5; Naphtali 2:5; 8:3–4; Asher 7:3; Dan 6:7; Judah 24:6; 25:5; Benjamin 9:2; 10:5, 10.

38. The Prescription of Heretics 7.

39. Apology 1. 46, from J. Quasten, *Patrology,* vol. 1 (Westminster: The Newman Press, 1950), p. 209.

40. For God as Father cf. Deut. 32:6; 2 Sam. 7:14; 1 Chron. 17:13; 22:10; 28:6; Isa. 63:16; 64:8; Jer. 3:4, 19; 31:9; Mal. 1:6; 2:10; Ps. 68:5; 89:26. For Israel as the "son" of God cf. Exod. 4:22; Isa. 1:3; Jer. 31:20; Hos. 11:1. For God's actions compared to those of a human father, cf. Deut. 1:31; 8:5; Mal. 3:17; Ps. 103:13; Prov. 3:12.

41. 2 Sam. 7:14; 1 Chron. 17:13; 22:10; 28:6; Ps. 89:26.

42. Isa. 63:16; Mal. 3:17; Ps. 103:13.

43. Deut. 32:8; Jer. 3:19.

44. Cf. Gen. 2:4b–7; 8:20–22; 9:18–19. These passages come from the J or Yahwist document, about 950 B.C.

45. Cf. also Isa. 63:16; 64:8; Jer. 31:20; Mal. 3:17; Hos. 1:10.

46. Jer. 3:4 and 3:19 are both problematic. Both could be construed as vocative, but are probably statements. On this problem cf. Jeremias, "*Abba,*" pp. 23–24.

47. Cf. Kittel and Friedrich, *Theological Dictionary of the New Testament,* 5:964–66.

48. For the term "Father" with respect to God in Hellenistic Judaism cf. the Apocalypse of Moses 35:2–3; 37:4; the Sibylline Books 3. 11. 278, 296, 550, 604, 726; 5. 11. 284, 328, 360, 406, 498, 500, 550; 3 Maccabees 2:21; 5:7; 6:4, 8; 7:6; Wisdom of Solomon 2:16; 14:3; Tobit 13:4.

49. From Robert H. Charles, ed., *The Apocrypha and Pseudepigrapha of the Old Testament,* 2 vols. (Oxford: Clarendon Press, 1963), 2:12–13. In the Pseudepigrapha cf. also Testament of Levi 18:6 and Testament of Judah 24:2. Since these passages both refer to a messiah, the word "Father" here may be a Christian interpolation.

50. From ibid., 1:513, with "Jahveh" changed to "Lord."

51. From P. Billerbeck, "Ein Tempelgottesdienst in Jesu Tagen," *Zeitschrift für die neutestamentliche Wissenschaft* 55 (1964):6.

52. b. Ta'an. 25b, as quoted by Jeremias, "*Abba,*" p. 25.

53. The Palestinian recension of the Eighteen Benedictions has the address "our Father" in the fourth and sixth benedictions; the Babylonian recension has it in the fifth and sixth benedictions. Jeremias regards all of these instances as later additions, because they lack parallels or because

they spoil the meter; cf. *"Abba,"* p. 26, n. 59. For the texts of these recensions cf. Strack/Billerbeck, 4 (pt. 1): 211–14.

54. Exodus Rabba 46 (101c), in Strack/Billerbeck, 1:393.

55. b. B.B. 10a (Bar.), in Jeremias, *"Abba,"* p. 19.

56. Targ. Isa. 63:16, in ibid., p. 20.

57. Yoma 8, 9, in P. Fiebig, *Jesu Bergpredigt* (Göttingen: Vandenhoeck & Ruprecht, 1924), p. 111.

58. Mark 8:38; 11:25; 13:32; 14:36. Luke 2:29; 6:36; 9:26; 10:21 (twice); 10:22 (three times); 11:13; 12:30, 32; 22:29, 42; 23:34, 46. Matt. 5:16, 45, 48; 6:1, 4, 6 (twice), 8, 14, 15, 18 (twice), 26, 32; 7:11, 21; 10:20, 29, 32, 33; 11:25, 26, 27 (three times); 12:50; 13:43; 15:13; 16:17, 27; 18:10, 14, 19, 35; 20:23; 23:9; 24:36; 25:34; 26:29, 39, 42, 53. These lists omit the Lord's Prayer and also statements attributed to the risen Lord.

59. For Mark, see preceding note.

60. Matt. 5:48–Luke 6:36; Matt. 6:32–Luke 12:30; Matt. 7:11–Luke 11:13; Matt. 11:25–Luke 10:21; Matt. 11:26–Luke 10:21; Matt. 11:27 (three times)–Luke 10:22 (three times).

61. Luke 2:49; 12:32; 22:29; 23:34, 46.

62. Matt. 5:16, 45; 6:1, 4, 6 (twice), 8, 15, 18 (twice), 26; 7:21; 10:20, 29, 32, 33; 12:50; 13:43; 15:13; 16:17; 18:10, 14, 19, 35; 20:23; 23:9; 25:34; 26:29, 42, 53.

63. In seven instances Matthew uses "Father" when the parallel verses in Luke do not have it; cf. Matt. 5:45; 6:26; 10:20, 29, 32, 33; 18:14. In two instances Matthew uses "Father" when parallel verses in Luke and Mark do not have it; cf. Matt. 12:50; 26:29. In two instances Matthew uses "Father" when the parallel verses in Mark do not have it; cf. Matt. 20:23; 26:42. There are no instances in which Luke or Mark has the word against the reading in Matthew.

64. Cf. the comment of J. Carmignac about the meaning of the word "Father": "For Christ, it expresses his Sonship within the Trinity; for Christians, it expresses their adoptive sonship" (*Recherches sur le "Notre Père"* [Paris: Letouzey & Ané, 1969], p. 64).

NOTES TO PAGES 57–82

1. For the text of this prayer, with references, see the appendix.

2. b. Berakoth 29b, in P. Fiebig, *Das Vaterunser* (Gütersloh: C. Bertelsmann, 1927), p. 37; also P. Fiebig, *Jesu Bergpredigt* (Göttingen: Vandenhoeck & Ruprecht, 1924), pt. 1, p. 116; pt. 2, p. 53.

3. Cf. J. Carmignac, *Recherches sur le "Notre Père"* (Paris: Letouzey & Ané, 1969); E. F. Scott, *The Lord's Prayer* (New York: Charles Scribner's Sons, 1951); P. Fiebig, *Das Vaterunser*; Strack/Billerbeck, vol. 1; A. Schlatter, *Das Evangelium nach Matthäus* (Stuttgart: Calwer Verlag, 1961); F. L.

Fisher, *Prayer in the New Testament* (Philadelphia: The Westminster Press, 1964).

4. Cf. J. Jeremias, *The Lord's Prayer* (Philadelphia: Fortress Press, 1964); E. Lohmeyer, *Our Father* (New York: Harper & Row, 1965); B. Noack, *Om Fadervor* (Copenhagen: G. E. C. Gad, 1969); K. G. Kuhn, *Achtzehngebet und Vaterunser und der Reim* (Tübingen: J. C. B. Mohr, 1950); R. E. Brown, "The Pater Noster as an Eschatological Prayer," in *New Testament Essays* (Milwaukee: The Bruce Publishing Company, 1965); E. von Dobschütz, "The Lord's Prayer," *Harvard Theological Review* 7 (1914): 293–321.

5. "Modus in 'sanctificetur' eandem vim habet quam in 'veniat' et 'fiat,' adeoque est rogatio, non doxologia expressa." Quoted by Lohmeyer, *Our Father*, p. 78.

6. Amos 2:7; Ezek. 20:39; 36:20, 21, 22; 39:7, 25; 43:7, 8; Isa. 57:15; Ps. 30:4; 33:21; 97:12; 103:1; 105:3; 106:47; 111:9; 145:21; 1 Chron. 16:10, 35; 29:16.

7. The forms of the verb vary: Ezek. 36:23 has the Piel of *qadesh*, while Isa. 29:23 has the Hiphil. L. Koehler explains the first as "put into the state of holiness" and the second as "treat as holy." Cf. L. Koehler and W. Baumgartner, *Lexicon in Veteris Testamenti Libros* (Leiden: E. J. Brill, 1958), p. 826. It is uncertain whether the Piel here has such a full causative and inchoative sense. Ezekiel probably believed that God's name retained its intrinsic holiness, even when this was not acknowledged among the peoples of the earth. The Piel, therefore, would mean "assert or manifest as holy." To the Piel correspond the Hithpael of Ezek. 38:23 ("I will show myself as holy") and the Hithpaal of the Kaddish ("sanctified be his great name").

8. Exod. 29:43; Lev. 10:3; 22:32; Num. 20:13; Ezek. 20:41; 28:22, 25; 36:23; 38:16; 39:27. The form of *qadesh* here is Niphal (reflexive or passive).

9. A possible exception is Exod. 29:43, which is textually uncertain.

10. Seder Eliyyahu Rabba 21 end, in Strack/Billerbeck, 1:411.

11. Siphra Lev. 18, 6 (339a), in ibid., p. 413.

12. Matt. 5:4, 6, 7, 9 (cf. Luke 6:21); Matt. 5:19; Matt. 7:1–2 (cf. Luke 6:37–38); Matt. 7:7–8 (cf. Luke 11:9–10); Matt. 10:19 (cf. Mark 13:11); Matt. 10:26 (cf. Mark 4:22; Luke 12:2); Matt. 10:30 (cf. Luke 12:7); Matt. 12:31–32 (cf. Mark 3:28; Luke 12:10); Matt. 12:37; Matt. 13:12 (cf. Mark 4:25; Luke 8:18; Matt. 25:29; Luke 19:26); Matt. 15:13, 24; 16:19; 18:18; 21:43; 22:14; Matt. 23:12 (cf. Luke 14:11; 18:14); Matt. 24:22; Matt. 24:40–41 (cf. Luke 17:34–35); Luke 11:51; 14:14.

13. Since the writings are later than the events that they describe, it is uncertain exactly when the Israelites first began to think of God as king. J. Gray connects the idea of the kingship of God with the Canaanite myth of Baal's conflict with the Sea and his assumption of kingship; cf. "The Hebrew Conception of the Kingship of God: Its Origin and Development," *Vetus Testamentum* 6 (1956):268–86.

14. Cf. Strack/Billerbeck, 1:172–73.

15. From Robert H. Charles, ed., *The Apocrypha and Pseudepigrapha of the Old Testament,* 2 vols. (Oxford: Clarendon Press, 1963), 2:647–49.

16. Ibid., pp. 421–22.

17. New Testament scholars differ widely in their interpretations of Jesus' understanding of the kingdom of God; but many, at least, would concur with the view of inaugurated eschatology presented here. A valuable survey of the problem is N. Perrin, *The Kingdom of God in the Teaching of Jesus* (London: SCM Press, 1963). In the study of the Lord's Prayer, it is especially B. Noack who follows along the lines laid down by J. Weiss and A. Schweitzer in arguing that Jesus regarded the kingdom as future. Noack recognizes that the "forces" of the kingdom are "already working," but only because the kingdom is in the imminent future rather than a distant future (*Om Fadervor,* p. 39). Noack seems to put too much emphasis on the element of discontinuity between present and future when he writes that the second petition "assumes precisely that God's kingdom is a break with this world, including life as it is lived here in faith" (ibid., p. 46).

18. Cf. Gerhard Kittel and Gerhard Friedrich, eds., *Theological Dictionary of the New Testament,* 9 vols. (Grand Rapids: Wm. B. Eerdmans, 1964–73), 3:54.

19. Mekilta Hashshira, pt. 3, on Exod. 15:2, in Fiebig, *Jesu Bergpredigt,* pt. 1, pp. 114–15.

20. Note especially that the idea of doing God's will, in Matt. 7:21 and 12:50, has no parallel in the similar material in Luke 6:46 and 8:21.

21. This interpretation is suggested by G. H. P. Thompson, "Thy Will be Done in Earth, as it is in Heaven (Matt. vi. 11): A Suggested Re-interpretation," *The Expository Times* 70 (Oct. 1958–Sept. 1959): 379–81.

22. Cf. Col. 1:20; Eph. 6:12; Rev. 21:1; possibly Col. 2:15; Eph. 1:10; 1 Cor. 15:24.

23. b. Berakoth 16b, in Strack/Billerbeck, 1:420.

24. Cf. the following verses in Matthew, many of which have parallels in Mark and Luke: 3:16, 17; 5:12, 34; 6:20; 11:23, 25; 14:19; 16:1, 19 (twice); 18:10, 18 (twice); 19:21; 21:25; 22:30; 23:22; 24:30, 31, 36; 26:64. Cf. further Luke 9:54; 10:20; 15:7, 18, 21; 16:17; 17:29; 18:13; 19:38. In Jesus' words, the idea that heaven contains forces hostile to God seems to appear only in the synoptic apocalypse (e.g., Matt. 24:29, 35 and parallels) and possibly in Luke 10:18 (if "from heaven" goes with "Satan fallen").

NOTES TO PAGES 83–113

1. Matthew uses aorist verbal forms throughout the Lord's Prayer; Luke usually has the aorist, but uses present stems in the petition for bread and in the clause "for we ourselves forgive. . . ." Some interpreters have argued that the aorist must refer to a single event, and thus they tend to limit the

meaning of the Lord's Prayer to God's final action at the close of history. The aorist in Greek, however, does not necessarily express a single event. It is essentially a punctiliar action-stem rather than a time-stem, and it means that an action or series of actions is viewed as a unity without reference to its duration. Perhaps the aorist forms in the Lord's Prayer can be understood best as examples of the complexive aorist; cf. H. W. Smyth, *Greek Grammar* (Cambridge: Harvard University Press, 1959), secs. 1923, 1927.

2. Mark 9:1 is often accepted as authentic on the grounds that the early church would not have created a "prophecy after the event" that had not proved to be true. N. Perrin, however, regards it as a Markan construction assuring the church that it would soon be released from persecution and suffering; cf. *Rediscovering the Teaching of Jesus* (New York: Harper & Row, 1967), pp. 16–20, 199–201.

3. Cf. B. M. Metzger, "How Many Times Does 'Epiousios' Occur Outside the Lord's Prayer?" in *The Expository Times* 69 (Oct. 1957–Sept. 1958): 52–54. According to Metzger, one possible example was a fragmentary fifth century papyrus of a householder's account book listing the purchase of provisions; this apparently had *epiousi*, but this reading is uncertain and cannot be checked since the manuscript itself was later lost. The other possible example was a Greek inscription from Lindos, on Rhodes, dated A.D. 22. Metzger believes, however, that the word here is a form of *eniausios* rather than *epiousios*. Cf. also the discussion by J. Carmignac in *Recherches sur le "Notre Père"* (Paris: Letouzey & Ané, 1969), pp. 121–22.

4. The meaning "necessary for existence" rests on a derivation from *epi* and *ousia*; this receives some support from the Peshitta, which has "for our need." The meaning "for today" would make *epiousios* equivalent to *epi tēn ousan (hēmeran)*; this receives some support from the Old Latin ("daily") and the Vulgate of Luke ("daily"). The meaning "for the coming day" would make *epiousios* equivalent to *epi tēn iousan (hēmeran)*; possibly this derivation was assumed by the Curetonian Syriac and the Sinaitic Syriac (on Luke), which have "continual." The meaning "for the future" would make *epiousios* equivalent in meaning to *to epion*; this receives some support from the Gospel according to the Hebrews and also apparently the Bohairic translation.

5. The first two meanings for *epiousios* derive it from *epi* and some stem from *einai*, "to be." The second two meanings rest on a derivation from *epi* and a stem of *ienai*, "to go." The objection is sometimes raised that *epi* loses its last letter when it is combined with a form of *einai*; this would give preference to a derivation of *epiousios* from *epi* and *ienai*. It is possible, however, that the word arose in popular usage that did not strictly observe the rules of word formation. Cf. Carmignac, *Recherches sur le "Notre Père,"* pp. 128–29; and Noack, *Om Fadervor* (Copenhagen: G. E. C. Gad, 1969), p. 149.

6. Berakoth vii 11a.35, in E. Lohmeyer, *Our Father* (New York: Harper & Row, 1965), p. 137.

7. 2 Baruch 29:5–6, 8, in Robert H. Charles, ed., *The Apocrypha* and *Pseudepigrapha of the Old Testament*, 2 vols. (Oxford: Clarendon Press, 1963), 2:497–98. For other examples of this type of symbolism in the Pseudepigrapha cf. 1 Enoch 62:14; 4 Ezra 6:49–52; Testament of Levi 18:8–11.

8. From the Rule of the Congregation, in M. Burrows, *More Light on the Dead Sea Scolls* (New York: The Viking Press, 1958), p. 395.

9. The Rule of the Congregation, ibid., p. 395.

10. R. Jacob, latter half of second century, in Aboth 4:21. Text in Charles, *Apocrypha and Pseudepigrapha of the Old Testament*, 2:706. Cf. also Aboth 3:20 (ibid., p. 702).

11. Midr. Esth. 1, 4, 86b, in Strack/Billerbeck, 4:1155.

12. Pes. 119b, 11; ibid., 4:1164.

13. R. Joshua, around A.D. 90, in Gen. Rabba 82; ibid., 4:1155.

14. Midr. Eccles. 1,9 (9b), in Strack/Billerbeck, 1:69.

15. The text of both quotations is available in *S. Hieronymi Presbyteri Opera*, Corpus Christianorum, Series Latina, vol. 78 (Turnholti: Typographi Brepols Editores Pontificii, 1958), p. 295. The translation of the first quotation is also given in *Gospel Parallels* ed., Burton H. Throckmorton (New York: Thomas Nelson & Sons, 1949), p. 25.

16. On the Gospel according to the Hebrews, cf. M. S. Enslin, "Nazarenes, Gospel of the," in George A. Buttrick, ed., *The Interpreter's Dictionary of the Bible*, 4 vols. (New York: Abingdon Press, 1962), 3:524. For the argument that *mahar* is only an attempt to explain the Greek text of Matthew, cf. P. Vielhauer in E. Hennecke, *New Testament Apocrypha*, vol. 1, ed. W. Schneemelcher (Philadelphia: The Westminster Press, 1963), pp. 118–46, especially pp. 134 and 142. For the view that *mahar* must represent the Aramaic wording as it lived on in continuous usage from Jesus' own time, cf. J. Jeremias, *The Lord's Prayer* (Philadelphia: Fortress Press, 1964), pp. 23–24. Jeremias recognizes that the Gospel according to the Hebrews, or the Gospel of the Nazarenes, is an Aramaic translation based on the Gospel of Matthew. But he argues that the translator simply stopped translating when he came to the Lord's Prayer. Instead, he put down the Aramaic words as he knew them from Aramaic-speaking Christians of his day.

17. Cf. Lohmeyer, *Our Father*, p. 161.

18. Cf. ibid.; also Jeremias, *The Lord's Prayer*, pp. 13–14, 27–28.

19. Tosephta Baba Qamma 9, 29f. (365 f.), in Strack/Billerbeck, 1:425.

20. b Taan. 25b, quoted by F. Hauck in Gerhard Kittel and Gerhard Friedrich, eds., *Theological Dictionary of the New Testament*, 9 vols. (Grand Rapids: Wm. B. Eerdmans, 1964–73) 5:562.

21. Cf. ibid. Hauck quotes the following passage from T. Qid. 1, 14 (sec. 336): "Because the individual is judged by the majority [of his works] . . . , man always appears to be in part righteous and in part guilty. If he keeps

a commandment, well with him, for he has . . . inclined the scale on the side of merit. . . ."

22. According to P. Fiebig, *Das Vaterunser* (Gütersloh: C. Bertelsmann, 1927), pp. 87–88; also I. Abrahams, *Studies in Pharisaism and the Gospels*, Second Series (Cambridge: The University Press, 1924), pp. 95–98.

23. Cf. Carmignac, *Recherches sur le "Notre Père,"* pp. 282–94; also his article, "Fais que nous n'entrions pas dans la tentation," *Revue biblique* 72, no. 2 (April 1965):218–26. The article by J. Heller is "Die sechste Bitte des Vaterunser," *Zeitschrift für Katholische Theologie* 25 (1901):85–93, especially pp. 90–93. Carmignac gives a French translation of Heller's article in *Recherches sur le "Notre Père,"* pp. 437–45.

24. b Berakoth 60b; Hebrew text in P. Fiebig, *Jesu Bergpredigt* (Göttingen: Vandenhoeck & Ruprecht, 1924) pt. 2, pp. 54–55.

25. J. Carmignac's explanation of the petition is the most satisfactory because it rests on an analysis of Semitic syntax, i.e., the negative with the Hiphil or (H)aphel. As soon as the Lord's Prayer was translated into Greek, the possibility of misunderstanding arose. For a discussion of various attempts throughout Christian history to interpret the petition, cf. Carmignac, *Recherches sur le "Notre Père,"* pp. 239–55.

26. According to Luke 8:13, in the interpretation of the parable of the sower, Jesus spoke of those who "believe for a while and in time of temptation fall away." This is also a reference to apostasy in time of suffering or persecution. The parallels in Matt. 13:21 and Mark 4:17, however, have "tribulation or persecution," indicating that Luke's wording is probably secondary. Elsewhere in the synoptics the noun *peirasmos* is used with reference to Jesus' own temptation or trials; similarly the verb *peirazo* is always used with reference to Jesus.

27. For this interpretation see especially Noack, *Om Fadervor*, pp. 93–95, and Lohmeyer, *Our Father*, pp. 204–208.

28. The Lord's Prayer uses "temptation" without the definite article, whereas Rev. 3:10 speaks of "the trial" or "the temptation." This usage suggests that in the Lord's Prayer, Jesus was not thinking of a specific temptation or specific category of temptation. Cf. Carmignac, *Recherches sur le "Notre Père,"* pp. 244–45, 280.

29. According to Lohmeyer, *Our Father*, p. 214. Lohmeyer himself, it should be noted, accepts the translation "the evil one."

30. According to ibid.; also Strack/Billerbeck, 1:422.

31. Matt. 5:37, 39 are other possible examples of "the evil one," with reference to the devil, but both are very doubtful.

32. For "the devil" in Jesus' words, cf. Matt. 13:39; 25:41; Luke 8:12. For "Satan," cf. Matt. 4:10; Matt. 12:26 (Mark 3:23, 26; Luke 11:18); Matt. 16:23 (Mark 8:33); Mark 4:15; Luke 10:18; 13:16; 22:31.

33. This is the case in 1 John 2:13, 14; 5:18. It is very probable in Eph. 6:16; 1 John 3:12; 5:19. It is also possible in John 17:15; 2 Thess. 3:3.

NOTES TO PAGES 114–119

1. Cf. E. von Dobschütz, "The Lord's Prayer," *Harvard Theological Review* 7 (1914):293–94.

2. Cf. G. Klein, "Die ursprüngliche Gestalt des Vaterunsers," *Zeitschrift für die neutestamentliche Wissenschaft* 7 (1906):39–40.

3. Cf. P. Billerbeck, "Ein Tempelgottesdienst in Jesu Tagen," *Zeitschrift für die neutestamentliche Wissenschaft* 55 (1964):7, 11.

4. Cf. Gerhard Kittel and Gerhard Friedrich, eds., *Theological Dictionary of the New Testament,* 9 vols. (Grand Rapids: Wm. B. Eerdmans, 1964–73), 2:294–95.

5. Cf. ibid. 2:245.

6. "Amen" was omitted from the doxology in the *Didache.* The critical apparatus of the Nestle text also indicates that it was omitted from two Old Latin manuscripts (g¹ and k) ; cf. E. Nestle, ed., *Novum Testamentum Graece,* 25th ed. (London: United Bible Societies, 1969), p. 13.

7. Cf. Strack/Billerbeck, 1:243.

8. Cf. ibid. 3:456–61.

NOTES TO PAGES 123–127

1. For the view that most of the Eighteen Benedictions were known in the first half of the first century A.D., cf. Strack/Billerbeck, 1:407–408. Billerbeck also stated, however, that only the first three and the last three benedictions existed in Jesus' day; cf. "Ein Synagogengottesdienst in Jesu Tagen," *Zeitschrift für die neutestamentliche Wissenschaft* 55 (1964) : 148. For the view that the Morning Prayer and the Evening Prayer very possibly existed in Jesus' time, cf. P. Fiebig, *Jesu Bergpredigt* (Göttingen: Vandenhoeck & Ruprecht, 1924), p. 118.

2. These are the oldest parts of the Kaddish, according to P. Fiebig, *Das Vaterunser* (Gütersloh: C. Bertelsmann, 1927), pp. 28–32. For the text cf. also Fiebig, *Jesu Bergpredigt,* pt. 2, p. 50.

3. This is the Palestinian recension of the Eighteen Benedictions, found in the Cairo geniza by S. Schechter and published in 1898, with the omission of some phrases which Dalman regarded as later additions. The translation follows the one in Strack/Billerbeck, 4:211–14.

4. According to Fiebig, *Jesu Bergpredigt,* p. 119 (Hebrew text in pt. 2, pp. 54–55).

5. According to ibid., pp. 118–19 (Hebrew text in pt. 2, p. 54).

Indexes

QUOTATIONS

AUTHORS

SUBJECTS